MW00387409

Rev. Cawthon-Freels's new book speaks to traditional church settings where scripture is try of scripture has made it imperative that i ancient truths that through the millennia have been misused to wound, alienate, and kill Queer people in the name of G-d and Jesus. This book is in every sense a life raft for the Queer Christian seeking some meaningful connection to scripture that is life-giving, liberating and affirming.

Using sound research and wonderful personal sources, Kali walks with the reader through what we know of as the Clobber Passages with a purpose to de-thorn the scriptures and reclaim them in the name of love from the Church's long history of homophobia. I think the readers will be educated on the truth behind these passages, often putting them at odds with their family's interpretation and their church's, but that is necessary if the Queer individual is grow in their faith. They can no longer simply swallow what is served to them without asking the hard contextual questions like who wrote this, who were they writing to, what did this word in Hebrew or Greek really mean during these ancient times?

What I appreciate most about this book is Kali's attention to the humanity of Queer folk. She offers insights into subjects such as chosen family and gender to give the reader context to locate themselves wherever they are along their own journey as a Queer person. This emphasis places scripture where it should be, as a sacred but fallible resource to point to the great mystery of our Creator. Kali resists making scripture or its interpretation an idol which allows the Queer Christian to learn about scripture without feeling as though it defines who they are to a loving G-d.

I pray this text and Kali's incredible witness serve as a balm to the wounds of the Queer community who carry the deep scars of a sick theology. Reclamation can bring liberation and healing.

Rev. Gator Blanchard
Associate Pastor, Unity Fellowship Owensboro, KY

Reclamation is the book all progressive churches need to read together! In it, Kali pushes beyond the important work of deconstruction (that we often get stuck in) and moves us toward building something new, generative, and redemptive. Kali interweaves careful scholarship, gentle spirituality, and the perfect dose of pop culture references! What emerges is a guide that dares us to think creatively and generatively about scripture that has done so much damage to so many people, and what these off-limits texts may have to offer us after all. The personal insight and vulnerability offered by Kali and by the authors of each of the "interludes" (brief essays by other LGBTQIA+ Christians) are a total gift to the church and the world. This is a courageous work of love that I highly recommend!

Rev. Natalie Webb
Senior Pastor, University Baptist Church, Austin, TX
Cofounder, Nevertheless She Preached

RECLAMATION

A Queer Pastor's Guide
to Finding Spiritual Growth in the
Passages Used to Harm Us

KALI CAWTHON-FREELS

© 2022

Published in the United States by Nurturing Faith, Macon, GA.
Nurturing Faith is a book imprint of Good Faith Media (goodfaithmedia.org).
Library of Congress Cataloging-in-Publication Data is available.

ISBN: 978-1-63528-166-8

Scripture quotations are from New Revised Standard Version Bible, copyright © 1989
National Council of the Churches of Christ in the United States of America.
Used by permission. All rights reserved worldwide.

Cover photo Aaron Burden on Unsplash.

Acknowledgements

This book was a labor of love. It would not exist without the cohort of people who stood behind me and supported me. It would be remiss of me to thank anyone but my wife Haley first, who put up with my long nights and endless questions like, "Hey, can you read this?" "What do you think?" You have always been my biggest cheerleader, and I don't know what I'd do without you.

A huge thanks to my contributors: Robert Arnáu, Autem Carter, Josh Carpenter, Haley Cawthon-Freels, Christy Dinkins, Grayson Hester, Ve Ivey, Teri King, Will Root, Cody J. Sanders, and Amanda West Wilkerson. Your stories elevated this devotional to something far more Spirit-infused than I could have created on my own. The way that the Divine speaks through each of you is a gift, and I am humbled that you would share it with me. Now, we get to share your gift with the world.

Thank you to my publisher Bruce Gourley, as well as the teams at Nurturing Faith and Good Faith Media. You've been in my corner from the day I sent the proposal. Thank you for giving this book a platform and believing in it just as much as I do.

Thank you to my church family at The Faith Community. As we're fond of saying, "I love y'all for real, fam." Thank you for trusting me to be one of your pastors, as well as for giving me a platform to teach content like this. I'm humbled by your embrace and I am honored to serve you.

Thank you to my besties, my forever gal-pal-sister-friends Amanda and Faith. I am always thankful for the family you are to me; that support and love has never been more evident.

And finally, thank you to the Creator, Christ, and Holy Spirit. Thank you for putting me in a position to bring these words together. I pray that they bless others as much as writing them blessed me.

Contents

Acknowledgements...v

Foreword...ix

Introduction: The Hot Stove 1

Chapter 1: A Place for Us...7
    Interlude: God's Good Pleasure..13

Chapter 2: The Value of Hospitality 15
    Interlude: Uplift and Love 21

Chapter 3: The Sacredness of Dignity..23
    Interlude: Redemption and Renewal...29

Chapter 4: Don't Be Deceived 31
    Interlude: Taking It Back 39

Chapter 5: A Beautiful Arc...41
    Interlude: No Shame...48

Chapter 6: Divine Certainty, Holy Mystery.......................................51
    Interlude: Wonder and Awe 57

Chapter 7: The Weight of Authority...59
    Interlude: On Divine Assignment..65

Chapter 8: Matters of the Heart...67
    Interlude: Grace in Love 73

Chapter 9: Proper Law 75
    Interlude: Risen Indeed...81

Chapter 10: Something's Missing 83
    Interlude: The Bigger Picture 89

Conclusion: Our Place at the Table 91

Epilogue: A Benediction Meal..97

Bibliography...101

Resource List..105

Foreword

Between the ages of six and ten, I played church in my backyard in a small chapel that my dad and paternal grandfather built for me, wearing a tiny robe and stole my paternal grandmother sewed for me, often accompanied by my maternal grandfather, who would assist me with services. Throughout childhood and adolescence, I rarely missed a Sunday in my actual small-town church either. It was a place of rich intergenerational relationship, joy, and beautiful music. In high school I carried a pocket-sized New Testament around with me in my jeans and never went to sleep at night without reading a passage of scripture. I went to college to study religion and seminary to prepare for ministry and graduate school to become a practical theologian.

I've loved the church and the Bible and the Christian tradition for as long as I can remember. I felt called into the vocation of ministry by a sense of the Spirit's luring that was affirmed by my congregation and nurtured by the ministers in my life.

For almost the entirety of this love affair with the church and my devoted practice of faith, I was also aware of my same-sex attraction, long before I knew any terms to describe my "sexual orientation." No one made a very big deal about "homosexuality" in the pulpit of my childhood church, but there was clarity on my part, nonetheless. I had an intuitive sense that others wouldn't respond well to this part of my sense of self. As I got older, I heard the message a little more clearly: this isn't something that a young man pursuing a call to ministry could do, could be, could even talk about.

For a long time, when it came to the intersection of my sexuality and faith, it was just me and the Bible, me and Jesus, me in prayerful exploration of my embodied life situated within this long tradition of faith. I needed to work things out, but I had to do so on my own. (A book like *Reclamation* would have really helped back then.)

Today, as a queer Baptist pastor, higher education chaplain, writer, and professor of pastoral theology and care, I hear this question a lot: Why did you stay in the church as a queer person? Not how did you navigate the tensions, or what resources helped you practice your faith as a queer person, or who supported you along the way, but why? It seems unfathomable to many—queer and cis/straight alike—that one could even find a reason to stay within a tradition that has so systematically and scrupulously worked to undo you and your queer siblings in faith.

To some degree, everyone—not just LGBTQIA+ people—should ask that question of their own life of faith: *Why do you stick with it?* Why continue to study the Bible knowing its long history of use in justifying varied forms of violence? Why continue to practice Christianity knowing its complicity in colonialism the world over? Why do you stay within a theological tradition that has been so frequently employed to sever our intimate relational ties to the larger web of life on an Earth now precipitously imperiled by human domination?

For queer people, staying in the church (or reinventing it), continuing to practice Christian faith (often with a carefully honed queer liberative lens), maintaining a devotional relationship with the text of scripture (sometimes after putting it down for a good long while) are not inevitabilities. It doesn't happen for us by getting caught in the cultural momentum or through acquiesce to the inertia of the status quo.

If you've never had to ask, *"Why do I stay in this church, denomination, or tradition?"* you've probably never experienced its more violent and violating edges. But queer people have. Those edges are hard to escape. When we stay—and it's understandably not something every LGBTQIA+ person is able to do—it's usually through some combination of prayerful discernment, diligent study, caring companionship, and faithful tenacity.

But staying is not the point. Living queer lives of faithfulness is an expression of beauty in the world. There's something of an art to it. There's no monolithic "queer Christianity." Nor should there be. We live our way into it, honing techniques and gathering treasures along the way that we can share with others. Queer liberation isn't just for LGBTQIA+ people, after all. It makes the life of faith better for everyone who has ears to hear and eyes to see and hearts prepared to learn and grow.

There are several practices for living at the intersection of LGBTQIA+ embodiment and Christian faith that are beautifully exemplified in this book, so carefully constructed by Kali Cawthon-Freels. I want to be sure you notice them as you read this incredible book:

Asking New, More Beautiful Questions

You don't always have to answer the questions you're given. I learned that after several years of doing the exhausting work that other people wanted me to do in order to justify my queer Christian existence and ministerial practice. I began to recognize that I had my own questions to ask, and those pursuits of inquiry were far more life-giving than the worn-out old questions of whether I could belong, or be ordained, or be in a same-sex relationship, etc. I could ask theological questions about the lessons of queer love and the life of queer faithfulness and what the Bible has to teach us about a whole lot more than where to draw the boundaries on who's in and who's out.

Rev. Cawthon-Freels and her LGBTQIA+ companions whose voices are represented in this book exhibit a love for the Bible. She looks upon these passages of scripture and develops meanings that the religious gatekeepers of the cishet status quo couldn't perceive in the texts. While many have looked at these texts and said, "Clearly, the message is that LGBTQIA+ people are living lives of sin." And others have carefully considered their context and said, "Not so fast! They don't quite say what you think they say about LGBTQIA+ people."

Reclamation doesn't stop there, however. This book asks bigger, more beautiful questions about these texts of scripture and about the life of faith for LGBTQIA+, straight, and cisgender people alike. Asking new questions results in faithful explorations we couldn't have imagined while being navigated by the restricting dictates of the old, well-worn queries.

Reclaiming Sources of Spiritual Sustenance on Our Own Terms

The souls of queer folk have long been sustained by the same sources of sacred wisdom used against us. But when we reclaim these sources of spiritual sustenance—whether prayer (after we've been told to "pray the gay away") or the Bible (after we've been told what it supposedly says about us)—we don't do so with naïveté. We know the source's power to harm, and we recognize its power to heal.

The Bible is one such source of harm and healing, and LGBTQIA+ people have (re)engaged scripture with a queer lens for a long time now. Rev. Cawthon-Freels takes this one bold step further: not just (re)claiming the Bible as a source of spiritual growth and faith development for LGBTQIA+ Christians, but pressing on to recover something of spiritual significance even in those passages used to "clobber" queer Christians.

This is a queer theological power move that restores the authority so frequently stripped from LGBTQIA+ people to read and interpret the Bible in its fullness with the fullness of our queer lives in view. Learn from this technique! It could save your faith, or maybe even your life.

Recognizing Queer Lives as
Sacred Sources of Wisdom

Finally, in foregrounding the narratives of ten other LGBTQIA+ people interspersed throughout her skillful readings of scripture, Rev. Cawthon-Freels makes one thing explicitly clear: LGBTQIA+ lives are sacred sources of wisdom. That is the ultimate act of reclamation in this text: reclaiming and proclaiming that the lives of LGBTQIA+ people are sacred, that we are beloved of God, that the church has more to learn from us than its establishment leaders dare to admit.

Queer folk are not out to "belong" within church structures that have marginalized us, or to finagle our way out of being condemned by the Bible, or to sit quietly by in self-satisfaction once we've been offered a place at the table. We're not even out to change the church. We're out to change the *whole world*. That is the calling of followers of Jesus: to realize a relational kindom forged in the shape of compassion, peace, and justice for every inhabitant of the Earth.

Blessings to you on that journey.

The Rev. Cody J. Sanders, Ph.D. (he/him/his)
Pastor, Old Cambridge Baptist Church American Baptist Chaplain,
Harvard University
Advisor for LGBTQ+ Affairs, Office of Religious, Spiritual, & Ethical Life, MIT
Cambridge, Massachusetts

Introduction

The Hot Stove

Growing up in the South, I learned many quippy sayings intended to quickly teach a lesson—short, sharp, Southern proverbs, if you will. "Don't count your chickens before they hatch." "Don't bite off more than you can chew." "Don't put all of your eggs in one basket." Of those quips, one has stuck with me the most over the years: "you only touch a hot stove once."

I don't think the lesson in that last proverb is terribly hidden here: if something or someone hurts you, you ought not interact with that person or thing again. But the way that my friends and family said that phrase indicated that there was another, unspoken lesson: if something hurts you, you'd be a fool to touch it again.

It's natural to run from things that hurt us. That survival instinct is hardwired into our DNA. But we often confuse harm with discomfort, so we end up avoiding important conversations simply because we don't want to be uncomfortable. That rationale is why many pastors stay away from challenging parts of the Bible altogether. It wasn't until I was in seminary that I discovered the stories of the rape and murder of the Levite's concubine, the sacrifice of Jephthah's daughter, and many other challenging narratives in the Bible. On one hand, I was shocked by the content of the stories. How could a book describing the love of God be so violent? How could a book about living like Jesus contain so much immorality? On the other hand, I was disappointed in my pastors. Why had none of my pastors ever discussed these passages? Weren't there lessons to be learned here as well? I assume that their fear of these passages (or, perhaps, their fear of mishandling them) led them to steer as far away from those passages as they could. Besides, there was the whole rest of the Bible to explore, right?

For many LGBTQIA+ Christians and allies, the infamous "clobber" passages (the handful of passages used by religious conservatives to demonize LGBTQIA+ people) elicit a similar response: stay far, far away. These verses haven't been used to make us uncomfortable; they've been used to cause us deep harm. How many times have we heard pastors scream from the pulpit that the sin of Sodom was sodomy? How many times have we had family members quote Leviticus and tell us that two men can't lie together? How many times have we heard well-meaning friends combat our lived experience with, "But what about Romans 1?" Some of us have had family members cut us off or kick us out of our homes, citing these verses as their justification for doing so. Others of us have heard these verses cited as the reasons why we couldn't participate in leadership at church and the reason why those churches denied us sacraments like marriage, Communion, baptism, or ordination. These conversations have left deep scars, wounds that we haven't forgotten. For some of us, those wounds have been deep enough to keep us out of the Bible altogether.

Even amidst the ever-increasing resources that prove that those passages aren't about same-sex relationships or gender expression, LGBTQIA+ persons and affirming pastors are hesitant to discuss these verses in small groups or preach them from pulpits. These passages are our hot stove: touch, and we're afraid we'll get burned again. If we do touch those verses, it's simply for the purpose of proving they have nothing to do with demonizing consensual same-sex relationships or expressions of gender identity. People like James Brownson, Matthew Vines, Justin Lee, Austen Hartke, and countless others have done tremendous work in this area. These voices have been essential in moving the conversation about LGBTQIA+ inclusion in the church forward, but I fear we've reached a plateau. We're stuck in this rut of saying, "That's not what these scriptures are about." If we stay here, we run the risk of losing any lessons to be learned from these texts. We can't keep defining these passages by what they aren't; we have to discover what they are.

A Shift

In the past couple of years, the needle has started to shift on LGBTQIA+ Christians' openness to scripture. Several LGBTQIA+ Christians and allies alike have striven to create Bible study materials that are affirming, inclusive, and true to scripture. Their tendency, however, has been to either avoid those aforementioned verses like the plague or to highlight the perspectives mentioned above (to indicate what they aren't about). Why would a progressive Bible study use verses that have been harmful to LGBTQIA+ lives for decades? Why go beyond the "these verses aren't about same-sex relationships or gender expression" dialogue? As LGBTQIA+ Christians and allies continue to return to the church and seek resources for spiritual growth, I invite us to ask a different question:

What does it mean to use these verses as tools for our spiritual growth and well-being? My aim is not to discuss how these verses are not intended to prove that being LGBTQIA+ is a sinful choice frowned upon by God. As I mentioned above, there are already several fantastic resources available that do that work justice. Instead, we will journey together to reclaim the lessons those texts have to offer us. For that reason, I will operate from a paradigm that assumes a fully affirming and inclusive theology from the start, as well as one that assumes my audience is operating from there as well. If you are not there theologically and have questions about how countless people have made this jump, I have included a list of resources at the end of this book that you may find helpful. This includes avoiding overly deep dives into translational nuances about specific words in some of the verses. For the ease of the reader, I scratch the surface on some of those word studies, but only for the sake of sticking to our task of finding the life-giving messages waiting for us in the text. For a more robust look at those translational nuances and deep word studies, I encourage you to reference the resources listed at the end of this book.

How to Use This Book

In this book, each "clobber" passage will have one chapter assigned to it, with the exception of Leviticus 18:22 and 20:13, which I paired together. All passages of scripture I quote will be from the New Revised Standard Version unless otherwise noted. I also encourage you to have your own Bible handy while you read so you can examine the text for yourself. At the start of each chapter, I'll begin with a story that will ease us into the theme of the verse. After that, we will briefly explore any contextual knowledge that will help us better understand the world of the authors. Then, we will focus on devotional-style reflections upon the text. After the reflection, I will leave several questions for you to consider as you examine how these verses provide spiritual instruction and comfort—yes, even comfort—to your own life. I will conclude each chapter with a prayer inspired by the theme of the verse and invite you to pray it as well.

In between each chapter, you'll find brief testimonies from other LGBTQIA+ Christians about what it means for them as queer Christians to reclaim scripture reading as a spiritual practice. Our community is diverse, and there are nuances in our sub-communities that each part of our community understands better than other parts do. I also believe that in order to better understand the Divine, we have to surround ourselves with as many people and perspectives as possible. If you surround yourself with people who only share your experiences, then you've surrounded yourself with mirrors and only see the same glimpse of God you see in yourself.

These interludes are vulnerable and thoughtful. I'm excited for you to hear the experiences of these fellow believers.

My hope is that this format will allow you to be as private or communal as you want to be in this process of rediscovering these passages. For some this will require breaks in between chapters—maybe for days or weeks—and perhaps you would prefer to meditate on those verses in solitude. That's fine, and I want to encourage you to do that. For others, you may want to audibly process the reflection questions with a group of trusted believers who are struggling with these verses the same way you are. If that's you, then embrace that feeling and start a small group on the topic. Maybe you want to journal about how a particular testimony resonates with your lived experience and you'd rather do that alone. Or perhaps a mixture of solitude and group discussion helps you absorb these lessons the most. No matter what method you choose, I want you to feel comfortable using this book in the way that enriches your soul the most. There is no wrong way to go about the process of reclamation.

But ... The Stove Is Hot

At this point, many of you may be wondering ... well, why? When we have a sacred scripture filled with thousands of instructive verses, why should LGBTQIA+ people and their allies even care about these? Why look for guidance in verses that have done nothing but cause pain to—burn—us and our loved ones for so long? Why bother?

Well, because I'm a sucker for redemption.

From January 2017 to July 2018, I had the pleasure to help my colleague and friend Rev. Adam Gray start a fully inclusive church plant in St Petersburg, Florida. In the early days, when the church plant was more of a vision than a reality, we sat at a table bouncing around ideas for names. Adam proposed the name Redeeming Church[1]—and I was hooked. While I loved the double entendre it presented (the fact that church needs to be redeemed for those whom the Church hurt juxtaposed against the reality that we believed we were actively redeeming what church can be), I loved the name because it aligned with my beliefs about the Gospel. As I would preach often in that congregation and many times since, I deeply believe that redemption is not a one-and-done deal; it's a never-ending process.

God has redeemed us. God will redeem us.

God is redeeming us even now, again and again and again.

If God is in the business of continually redeeming us, then I believe God has to be in the business of continually redeeming God's misused, misquoted, cherry-picked Word. If God wasn't in the business of redeeming God's Word, then God would have stopped speaking through the Bible long ago—when it was used to defend slavery; when it was used to legalize segregation; when it was used to vilify interracial marriage; when it was used to justify the Holocaust; when it is used to promote violence against women; when it is used to deny sanctuary to refugees; and now, when it is used to harm LGBTQIA+ persons.

If God wasn't in the business of redeeming God's Word, the only responsible Christian response would have been to ditch the Bible a long, long time ago.

So yes, the stove is hot, but it wasn't being used properly. When a stove is used improperly, it becomes something terribly dangerous. It can cause serious harm to the one using it and anyone in proximity to that person. Improperly used stoves have been the culprits of upturned lives, destroying any safety or security someone has. Not only that, improperly used stoves cause deep burns and, if the damage is deep enough, it can claim a life. Those of us in the LGBTQIA+ community know that all too well.

But when it's used correctly, a stove can be used to make something extraordinary. It can be used to create a meal for a table, around which people from all walks of life can talk, laugh, and be nourished. It can elicit feelings of welcome and warmth, creating an atmosphere of love and inclusion. When a stove is used properly, it feeds not just the body, but the soul.

You may not be ready to engage this particular stove because of how deeply it has hurt you—and that's okay. As we deal with the damage that these verses have done, we each have our own healing journey to walk. For some of you, the conversation this book provides will be a healing balm; for others, encountering these passages again may be too deep a reminder of the pain they've caused you. Your path to healing may not include revisiting these passages or reading this book, and that's okay. Engage both God and your own inner wisdom before choosing to embark on this journey.

To the straight cisgender folks who may have picked this book up on a whim, you may feel like you're "on the outside looking in" while reading the experiences of the queer folks who contributed to this book. I want to encourage you to read it anyway. Treat this as an opportunity to learn about your siblings in Christ and how you might be a better sibling for them. You might even find some healing for yourself within these pages.

If you—queer folk or cishet ally—choose to take this path, know that we are not starting at ground zero. Thanks to many fantastic theologians and pastors, we know that those verses have been used improperly for far too long, and we can examine them with new eyes. We can see lessons full of love instead of hate. We can see instruction instead of condemnation. Together, we can discover a message around which people from all walks of life can talk, laugh, and be nourished.

Yes, the stove is hot. But we have oven mitts. Let us explore and be nourished.

Note

[1]Redeeming Church has since merged with another like-minded ministry and renamed themselves the Circle of Faith. If you're in the Tampa Bay area and are looking for a fully LGBTQIA+ affirming ministry, I encourage you to check them out (https://circle.faith/).

Chapter 1

A Place for Us

"So God created humankind in their image, in the image of God they created them; male and female God created them."—Genesis 1:27

Those of us in the LGBTQIA+ community don't often see images in media that we resonate with; if we do, the character is often a side character provided for comedic relief. Thankfully, this reality is changing over time, but, because the opportunities are so rare, we latch onto the parts of media that make us feel seen. Many of these parts tend to come to us as songs from musicals, as theatre has long been a refuge for us. Over the years, songs like "Defying Gravity" from *Wicked*, "Seasons of Love" from *Rent*, "I Am What I Am" from *La Cage aux Folles*, and countless others have become anthems for our community as they provide words to our lived experience. These words are words that we often struggle to find ourselves, but the musicians seem to capture for us perfectly and effortlessly.

In recent years, I don't think any song has done that better than "This Is Me" from *The Greatest Showman*. In the film, Lettie Lutz, a bearded woman, leads other circus performers in boldly singing this song in front of a mob that is carrying torches, brandishing pitchforks, and screaming "freaks" and "go home" at the group. In the face of all that hate, the circus performers stare the protestors in the eye and sing, "I won't let them break me down to dust/ I know that there's a place for us/ For we are glorious … I'm not scared to be seen/I make no apologies/this is me."[1] Because these words are sung by a group of people who could not be easily categorized by their society, led by a woman who does not fit the stereotypical presentation of a woman, LGBTQIA+ folks have latched onto this song like the lifeline it is to us. I remember sitting on my couch sobbing the first time I watched this scene because I felt so seen. I still can't watch this part of the film without tearing up.

The character Lettie Lutz was based on the real-life bearded lady Annie Jones Elliot, who actually traveled with the Barnum and Bailey's Circus in the late 1800s. She was a hairy child from birth and, by the age of five, had sideburns and a mustache. Annie's mother approached Barnum and Bailey to see if she could be part of their "curiosities" exhibit, and they paid Lettie a then-luxurious $150 a week to be part of the cast of performers. As Annie grew older, she decided that she didn't want to be simply stared at; she wanted to be a performer. She trained to become a vocalist and had a wealth of natural talent. She was known throughout the United States and Europe for her magnificent singing; it seems only fitting that the character Lutz would also have a phenomenal voice.[2]

Keala Settle, the actress who played Lutz and sang "This Is Me," said that she got the inspiration for her character's personality from activist Harnaam Kaur, a present-day bearded woman who raises awareness about the complexities of polycystic ovarian syndrome (PCOS), of which thick, stubbly hair growth is a side effect. Kaur regularly posts pictures on social media proudly showcasing her full beard, hoping to generate body positivity amongst those who have conditions like PCOS.[3] As someone with PCOS myself, posts like Kaur's remind me that I'm not alone. I have always had thick hair all over my body (my new doctor even commented in a recent visit that I'm "really good" at growing hair). I have a little chin-beard that I've stopped fighting because, well, it's just a part of my body.

Women like Jones, Lutz, Kaur, and even me are easy targets for the microaggression of misgendering because we're what lesbian comedian Hannah Gadsby calls "man at a glance."[4] We don't look the way women are "supposed" to look; we don't fit into the mold of womanhood as society dictates it. If we rely on a binary understanding of gender to show us where we fit, then there isn't a place for us. Are we not glorious?

As we dig into Genesis 1:27, it's important to understand the context of Genesis 1 as a whole. While its literary setting is, well, the beginning of time, it was not written down until about the 6th Century BC, during the Babylonian Exile.[5] Up to this point, the events in Genesis would have been passed down as oral tradition. During the Exile, the Israelites were scared. They didn't know if or when they'd be able to return to The Promised Land. They were in the midst of chaos, and their future as a nation was incredibly uncertain. By beginning the book of Genesis with God creating order out of chaos, the authors were reminding the Israelites that God would create order out of their current chaos, too. If God could order the universe, God could order their lives. With that context in mind, let's jump into the text itself.

Chapter 1 starts by setting the stage for the nothingness that is present and introduces us to God as this Spirit hovering above the waters. As the verses progress, the author describes all the things that God makes: light and dark, fish of the sea and animals of the land, and so on. Each day God creates new categories for where things should go in the created order. Everything has a place; everything belongs. Sounds nice, right? Especially to a group of people who are in the midst of their own chaos, a story that explains things with such certainty and order could be a great comfort.

In our lived experience, we find that it's not always that easy to describe creation. In his work, transgender theologian Austen Hartke constantly points out that there are things in nature that don't fit neatly into the binary-based categorization system the book of Genesis describes. Is a marsh "land" or "sea"? How do we categorize the time of day when the sun is still in the sky but we can also see the moon? What do we do with fish that change gender based on need (more on that in Chapter 6)? And—Hartke's favorite thing to highlight—where in the world would the authors of Genesis put the platypus?[6] None of these bits of creation are terribly rare or exotic; most of us have probably seen at least one of these things in the past week. Since these things don't neatly fit into the binary-based categories described in Genesis, did God make a mistake when creating them? Or are they sinning simply through their mere existence?

Hartke and others argue that the use of binaries in the first chapter of Genesis isn't to set up an exclusive, concrete organizational system, but to simply highlight the extreme ends of the spectrum; of course God made everything in between. In a conversation, Hartke's friend M Barclay said, "When we call God the Alpha and the Omega, we don't just mean that God is the first and the last. We mean that God is everything from the first to the last."[7] When we focus only on the extreme ends of the spectrum, we lose the nuances of the spectrum itself.

> **A Word About Gender**
>
> Before White colonizers invaded, innumerable indigenous cultures around the world recognized the existence of more than two genders. In fact, some Native American tribes recognized as many as five genders, and many of the people we would call nonbinary had places of honor and authority within their society.[8] To learn more, check out some of the sources I've included in the resource list.

We see this nuance in God through the life and personhood of Jesus Christ. In the beginning of the Gospel of John—the style of which is intentionally reminiscent of Genesis 1—it says, "In the beginning was the Word, and the Word was with God, and the Word was God. He was in the beginning with God ... And the Word became flesh and lived among us, and we have seen his glory." So then comes the age-old question: Was Jesus divine or human? This question has been debated for centuries and we could spend the rest of this book and then some looking at the various arguments. As fascinating as that particular rabbit hole is, I'll focus on one argument by a friend that adds the most clarity I've ever seen on this idea. My friend and colleague Grayson Hester has said to me and others on multiple occasions that Jesus was both, neither, and more. Jesus was nonbinary because he doesn't fit on either extreme. Jesus wasn't simply human or simply divine. He was a mixture that exists beyond the binary of "human/divine" that we've created in order to try and make sense of the chaos that is a growing spirituality. Jesus doesn't fit into any category, but we need him to in order for us to understand him better. So, we made the categories and forced Jesus to fit wherever we thought was best, even if the fit wasn't perfect.

Even though Jesus himself would not fit neatly into the categories described in Genesis 1, I'd be willing to bet no Christian of any stripe would say that Jesus is an abomination to God.

If God made everything—including the in between spaces that go unnamed in the book of Genesis—why did the authors leave the rest of the spectrum out? Surely, they saw the sun and the moon in the sky at the same time like we do sometimes. Based on the patterns in the text, it certainly seems to be an intentional choice on the part of the authors to leave those in between spaces out.

When you're teaching something—especially a new thing—it's my experience that binaries are easier for people to learn. Musicians like Broadway performers know this well. When we first learn dynamics and tempos, we are taught a binary: loud and soft, fast and slow. The binary is clear; if it's not soft, it's loud; if it's not fast, it's slow. But as we develop our craft more, we learn nuance. Yes, there's loud and soft, but there's also slightly soft and slightly loud, blow-the-roof-off-the-joint loud, and barely-above-a-whisper soft. The same is true with tempo. Yes, there's fast and slow, but there's American march fast (120 beats per minute) and British march fast (112 beats per minute), there's funeral dirge slow, and there's so fast that "the conductor can only signal every fourth beat" fast. If we were presented with all of that nuance as beginner musicians (especially child musicians), I daresay no one would make it past their first year learning music because they all would have lost patience. The nuances would have been too chaotic, too much all at once. The binary is a good place to start because it sets clear expectations. If we stay in that binary, though, we will never advance as musicians. All the music you listen to would be rather boring if the only choices were loud/soft and fast/slow.

Later scripture writers understood this concept well. One of my favorite verses of all time is Hebrews 5:13-14: "For everyone who lives on milk, being still an infant, is unskilled in the word of righteousness. But solid food is for the mature, for those whose faculties have been trained by practice to distinguish good from evil." Just before this verse, the author tells the audience that they need "milk not solid food" because they need to relearn the fundamentals (which we all need to do now and again). But the overarching lesson here is that once we've got the fundamentals of faith down, we can't stay in the fundamentals if we expect to grow deeper in our faith. Nuance is like meat or a plant-based protein. It's complex and takes your body longer to digest, but it is full of more nutrients than milk alone could ever provide. In the same way, we need to train our spirits to better digest the complex proteins of our faith.

The word "genesis" means "beginning," and that's what the book of Genesis should be: a beginning. A binary understanding of God and spirituality should be the beginning of our faith, but it should not be where our faith stays. If we let our faith stay here, then we're just drinking milk—we won't grow anymore.

What can we learn here? While there are so many beautiful lessons to be learned from this text, two things stand out to me. First, we have to allow our faith to grow, to move onto more complex practices and thoughts, in order to better understand the nuances of being a faithful Christian. We've got to graduate from holy milk to sacred complex proteins if we ever hope to grow into better, more faithful disciples.

Secondly, and more importantly, all of humanity is created in God's nonbinary image. In the diversity of gender throughout the world, we see a small glimpse of the diversity that exists within God's own self. None of us can grasp the idea of the image of God by simply looking in a mirror, because we are each but one fragment of God's image. We have to embrace as many different people as possible to get a fuller picture. Because every single one of us is made in God's image, we all belong in the divine portrait. We all have a seat at the table. We all have a place in the Kindom of God, just as we are.

There is a place for us, for we are glorious.

As you continue to meditate on this verse, I want to encourage you to take a moment to examine the image of God within yourself. You, child of God, are made in God's image. You are holy; within you, you contain divinity. Make no apologies for who you are, for you are fearfully and wonderfully made.

Reflection Questions

- What are some of the "in between" places where you've felt the Divine? What about places beyond the binary altogether?

- Think of a chaotic time in your life. How did God bring order to that chaos?

- How does eliminating binary thinking help you see God, Jesus, and the Holy Spirit differently?

- Where are the current "complex protein" places in your own spiritual journey right now? How are they helping you grow?

Prayer

Lord of all creation, of every people of every nation, grow in us a spirit of acceptance. Let us embrace your image wherever we find it. Help me embrace the image of you that exists in me, just as I am, especially on the days when others make me feel otherwise. In the same fashion, help me accept your image in others, especially those who hold within them a different image of you than I have. They are glorious, and just as worthy of my love. Amen.

Interlude: God's Good Pleasure

Therefore, my beloved, just as you have always obeyed me,
not only in my presence, but much more now in my absence,
work out your own salvation with fear and trembling;
for it is God who is at work in you, enabling you both to will
and to work for God's good pleasure.—Philippians 2:12-18

After seminary, I sold all my commentaries, ditched all my books about the Bible, and pared down my library with a heavy heart full of defeat and bitterness. I was about to come out of the closet following a time at a far-too-conservative-for-me institution, and I realized that my job prospects as a minister were slim to none. I was grieving both the loss of the potential for employment but also the loss of my faith tradition—I was raised Southern Baptist, and I had finally decided to choose my own health, sanity, and sexuality over the confines of the tradition I was raised in.

But I sold my library for more reasons than just grief. I felt that I would never touch the Bible again—why should I when all it had ever brought me was grief and pain? I felt that the Bible was a book for straight people; the liberation and hope it could bring was for people whose sexuality did not get in the way of their hopes and dreams. What could the Bible offer me other than more suffering?

Fortunately God was not at all perturbed by my sexuality and did not operate within the confines I had made for God. It took years to work through all the pain I had faced, but God's patience outlasted my suffering. Eventually I allowed myself space to listen to the Bible again, and I realized that there was no reason why I should allow the institutions that were bent on excluding me and others to define what the Bible meant. Why shouldn't I follow Paul's instructions in Philippians 2 and work out my own salvation? Why shouldn't I allow God to do the work of joining with me in finding God's good pleasure for my life, a good pleasure that does not exclude my sexuality?

Let me encourage you to embrace this book about the Bible, to allow God to work outside the frameworks you have established. God doesn't pay a bit of attention to your frameworks—God is too big for them, and so are you.

Josh Carpenter (he/they)
A Queer Christian

Notes

[1] Keala Settle and The Greatest Showman Ensemble, "This is Me," by Benj Pasek and Justin Paul, recorded 2017, track 7 on *The Greatest Showman: Original Motion Picture Soundtrack*, Atlantic, digital album.

[2] "Annie Jones—The Esau Woman," *The Human Marvels*, https://www.thehumanmarvels.com/annie-jones-the-esau-woman/ (accessed May 16, 2021).

[3] Angelica Florio, "The Real Activist Who Inspired The Greatest Showman's Bearded Lady Is So Inspiring," *Bustle*, December 22, 2017, https://www.bustle.com/p/the-actor-who-plays-the-bearded-lady-in-the-greatest-showman-has-a-message-about-self-love-7630055 (accessed May 16, 2021).

[4] Hannah Gadsby, *Hannah Gadsby: Nanette*, directed by Jon Olb and Madeleine Parry, *Netflix*, 2018. *Netflix*, https://www.netflix.com/title/80233611.

[5] Walter Brueggemann, *Genesis*, Interpretation: A Commentary for Teaching and Preaching, ed. James Luther Mays (Atlanta: John Knox Press, 1982), 24-35.

[6] Austen Hartke, "The Bible and Transgender Christians," The Reformation Project Symposium in Chicago, IL, October 28, 2017, *YouTube*, 41:44, https://www.youtube.com/watch?v=zs_Baw-5ydg (accessed May 14, 2021).

[7] Ibid.

[8] Centennial College, *Our Stories: First Peoples of Canada*, Pressbooks, https://ecampusontario.pressbooks.pub/indigstudies/chapter/gender-identities/ (accessed June 25, 2021).

Chapter 2

The Value of Hospitality

"And they called to Lot, 'Where are the men who came to you tonight? Bring them out to us, so that we may know them.'"—Genesis 19:5

When I was an undergraduate student, I had the opportunity to go on tour with the premiere choir of the university. I didn't go as a vocalist, but as an instrumentalist—I played clarinet (considering all the music talk in the previous chapter, are you surprised?) and they needed a small ensemble to accompany some of their pieces. It was a week-long endeavor comprising about 50 of us. We traveled all over the Southeast for this tour: Chattanooga, Atlanta, Charleston, and tons of smaller towns in between. When we weren't performing, we were exploring the cities, getting to know our classmates more, or laughing at student-made videos that debuted on the bus during particularly long stretches of travel. That experience is one of my fondest college memories.

We were paying for most of the trip expenses ourselves and, as broke college students, staying in hotels every night would have made the trip impossible for most of us. To keep the cost of the trip down, the choir director coordinated with each of the churches where we'd be performing; each church rallied together a brigade of members to host a handful of students each. Let me say that again—the members of these churches agreed to host college students that they had never met. Some may call it crazy; others may call it an act—or even a giant, bounding leap—of faith. Whatever you call it, we gave thanks at every home because each home we got to stay at was one less hotel bill. Those church members made the trip possible.

Many of these families gave us much more than a room for the night. In one city, one of the springs on my clarinet broke; without hesitation, one of the host moms drove me to the best music shop in Atlanta to get it repaired. In another town, a sweet elderly woman made me and one of my classmates homemade peaches and cream, using her special canning peaches that she had been saving for a special occasion; she even brought out her special china to serve it on. In another town, one family hosted six of us, created a welcome basket full of snacks, drinks, and games for us to play, and gave us free rein of their game room in the basement. The list of thoughtful deeds could go on and on. At every home we went to we weren't simply housed. We were welcomed.

As strange as an introduction about welcome may seem in a chapter about Sodom and Gomorrah, I think you'll find that these stories provide the perfect foil for the reflections ahead. In the name of welcome, I invite you to curl up with a comfy blanket and your favorite warm beverage as we dig into these lessons together.

To understand the sad tale of Sodom and Gomorrah, we have to go back a chapter to Genesis 18. Many people know this chapter by the story at the middle of it: God promising Abraham that Sarah would have a child a year later, as a reward due to Abraham's faithfulness. If they don't know this chapter by that story, then most people know it by the story at the end of the chapter: Abraham pleading to God on Sodom's behalf to spare the city from destruction. For our purposes, we need to go to the beginning of the chapter to an often-overlooked story about hospitality. You're welcome to read the story of Genesis 18:1-8 from your own Bible, but I'll also provide the KPV (Kali's Paraphrased Version) below.

One day, Abraham was tending to his flock when he saw three men approaching his camp. It was hot, and Abraham feared that the men were tired from their travels. He ran out to meet them, bowed in front of them, and insisted that they stay with him for dinner so they could rest. The men agreed that the rest would do them good and decided to take Abraham up on his offer. Abraham ran back to his tent, told Sarah that guests were coming, and asked her to make a ton of bread. He then went hurriedly back to his herd, selected the finest calf, and slaughtered it for a meal. As the men sat under the shade of a tree, Abraham provided them water so they could wash their weary, dirty feet. When Sarah finished cooking, the men ate a lavish meal of bread, meat, and milk

A Word About Welcome

In the LGBTQIA+ community, you will be hard-pressed to find someone who has not been on the receiving end of radical exclusion: be it from families, churches, or jobs. That is precisely why the LGBTQIA+ folks I know have been some of the most welcoming people I've known in my life. I will never forget the organist at the church I attended while in seminary. Every year, he and his husband would throw an elaborate Christmas party— catered snack bar, endless wine, and Christmas caroling together around his in-home organ. One year, I commented to him how much I looked forward to this party every year, and he responded, "For some folks, this is the only Christmas they get. So, we want to make sure it's special for them."

with curds. Abraham made sure the men were well cared for before they continued their travels.

In this story, Abraham serves as a model of what radical hospitality looks like—or is it all that radical? If you look at Genesis 24:28-32, Leviticus 19:33-34, Deuteronomy 10:17-22, countless other Hebrew Bible stories, and innumerable stories from other Ancient Near Eastern cultures of that same time, hospitality was the societal norm.[1] Hebrew people of the time had a hospitality code that was deeply intertwined in their religious practices. Providing hospitality to strangers was expected—we could fill an entire chapter with citations of times God told the Israelites to care for the foreigner. While we might think hospitality of that nature as pretty radical, Abraham was doing exactly what his culture expected him to do.

Even so, Abraham went out of his way to make sure that the men weren't simply housed, but welcomed. Instead of serving day-old bread, he asked Sarah to bake fresh bread. Instead of grabbing any cow from the herd, he selected the finest one for their meal. Abraham could have provided the bare minimum in order to show hospitality to these strangers and still meet the cultural expectations, but he went above and beyond to ensure that they felt like the most highly honored guests.

At this point, you may be thinking, "This is a nice teaching, Kali, but what does any of this have to do with the story of Sodom and Gomorrah?"

Everything.

Now, flip the page to Genesis 19. Here, we see Lot, Abraham's nephew, take the center stage. Lot notices two men (at least, he thought they were—but more on that in a moment) traveling toward the city. Night would be falling soon, so he met the men on the road and invited them to stay the night with him, likely influenced by the example his uncle Abraham set for him as he was growing up. At first the men declined Lot's offer, but Lot all but begged them to stay. They finally agreed and followed him to his house. As the night wore on, men from all over the city of Sodom came to Lot's door, demanding to see these strangers. Not only did they want to see these strangers, they wanted to harass these strangers—even rape them. Lot protected them and offered his virgin daughters to the crowd instead to appease their desires (Yikes!). The men of the city wouldn't have it; they wanted to ravage these strangers. Just as the crowd was turning into a mob, the strangers pulled Lot back inside the house and locked the door. The men, who were really angels in disguise, blinded the men of the city and warned Lot to get his family and escape from the city because God was going to destroy it. After some back and forth about where they should go, Lot and his family fled to the neighboring town of Zoar. Once Lot and his family were safe, God destroyed Sodom and Gomorrah. The next morning, Abraham could see the smoke of the distant ruins from his camp.

Read in isolation, as these stories often are, these two stories teach little. Read together as a couplet as intended though, these stories teach the value of hospitality. Abraham's radical hospitality is juxtaposed against the radical hostility of the men of Sodom.[2] Where Abraham sought to restore the travelers, the men of Sodom sought to ravage them.

Moreover, these stories teach how much God values hospitality. In Genesis 18, God rewards Abraham's radical hospitality with the promise of a son. This was the equivalent of God promising Abraham that Abraham's lineage would continue and his legacy would live on in the life of his son and his son's children; it was like promising Abraham immortality because his legacy wouldn't die. In Genesis 19, God doesn't just punish the men of Sodom for their radical hostility—God burns the city to the ground. The lack of hospitality the city shows is so shameful that God deems the entire city unworthy of existence.

That shame is echoed throughout the entirety of the Hebrew Bible. Isaiah says that the offerings of Sodom and Gomorrah were meaningless to God due to their lack of care for the stranger (Isaiah 3:9). Jeremiah claims anyone who "lives a lie" or "strengthens the hand of evil doers" is just as detestable as the citizens of Gomorrah (Jeremiah 23:14). Only Ezekiel, though, explicitly names the sins of Sodom and Gomorrah: they were prideful, arrogant, and refused to help the poor and needy. To put it simply, they failed at hospitality and showed no compassion for the stranger (Ezekiel 16:49).[3]

The lesson of Sodom and Gomorrah is a chilling warning of how much God values hospitality. It serves as a warning that God loves all of God's children and will not tolerate the mistreatment of the divine creation. The Hebrew Bible is full of instruction after instruction about how God cares for the orphan, the widow, and the stranger. Not only does God care about them, but God instructs Israel to care for them throughout the entirety of the Hebrew Bible.

The idea of offering hospitality is so important to the Ancient Israelite traditions that it even extends into the New Testament. When Jesus finished teaching the crowd of more than 5,000 people, he showed them hospitality by feeding them. When Jesus and his 12 closest disciples gathered in the upper room, he showed them hospitality by washing their feet. When Jesus said, "Whatever you do to the least of these, you do to me," he was saying that we should greet and treat strangers the same way we would Christ himself. As a devout Jewish man, Jesus was pulling from the morals of stories like Genesis 18 and 19 when he was teaching his disciples to care for their neighbor, the widow, and the orphan.

As challenging as this story is to read, it is an encouragement, too. As much as it inspires us to be more hospitable in our own lives, it also reminds us that God expects others to welcome us with that same hospitality, too. That just as much as you should prepare a meal for a stranger, you are worth a stranger preparing you a meal. And just as much as you should welcome others with open arms and affection, you deserve to be welcomed with compassion, too. In both stories, we can insert ourselves into the role of the host or the visitor and see clear expectations of how we should be treated. Just because you are to be a hospitable person does not mean you are to be treated as a doormat yourself; other Christians are to treat you with the same level of hospitality. It all comes back to the golden rule: "Do unto others as you would have them do unto you."

As you reflect on these stories, I invite you to make hospitality a pillar of your faith, both in how you give it and how you receive it. We must treat our neighbors like children of God they are, but we must also accept the same treatment in return. So, keep a pot of water on and at the ready to brew some fresh coffee or tea. Who knows? You may find yourself entertaining angels more often than you think.

Reflection Questions

- Think of a time you offered someone hospitality. What did that hospitality look like?

- Think of a time when you were on the receiving end of radical hospitality. How did you react?

- Has there been a time when you denied hospitality to someone? Why?

- What makes receiving hospitality from others hard?

- What can you apply from this story to live a life more reflective of radical hospitality? How can you keep yourself accountable to applying that action?

Prayer

Lord of all creation, of every person of every nation, grow in us a hospitable spirit. Let us see you and ourselves in every soul we meet and let us welcome them as your child and our sibling. May we see no strangers, but only neighbors made in your image and worthy of love. And by that same token, we ask that we may be received by strangers with that same brand of radical hospitality. Amen.

Interlude: Uplift and Love

Growing up as a closeted cis-passing queer girl in a traditional Black, National Baptist church had its bittersweet privileges. My leadership roles and ideas for moving the ministry forward were approved by my pastor, while my close queer friends who were out and proud were forced out of their leadership positions. I was furious with my religious community and felt that many of its leaders failed the foundational test of love, which is essentially supposed to be the core of any Christian's beliefs. Once I decided that I did not have to abide by indoctrinated traditions in order to be loved by God and proclaimed that love would be the core to my belief system, I was able to take all I had learned from Sunday School, Bible study, VBS, revivals and morning worship services and use scripture to find the best way to navigate my spiritual journey as openly transparent queer Black woman.

Ways to help other young Christians—who face multiple realities due to their intersectionality—feel comfortable in finding their own spirituality became easier to navigate as I experienced more of what life had to offer. While pursuing my doctorate a few years ago, I was inspired to study the spirituality experiences of Black undergraduate women. During my study, I found that, although all my student participants found their own spirituality as young adults, much of the internalized messages they received from their family and religious communities weighed heavily on how they defined their new spirituality. This research study helped me realize how I can use scripture to do good work for my various communities (i.e., Black, POC, LGBTQIA+, academia, young adults, women, etc.), and allow time for self-healing to take place while I work through my own spirituality experiences.

Because of my belief in Matthew 22:36-40, "The Greatest Commandment" (called "The Golden Rule" throughout my childhood), I treat everyone with decency, respect and love, no matter their beliefs or backgrounds. Because of my hope in Luke 6:35-38, I do not seek revenge on people who have spoken ill against me because they do not like "all sides of me." Because of the 23rd Psalm, I realize that God prepares a table before me in the presence of those who have spoken ill of me. Because of my belief in Ephesians 4:15, James 1:19, and Proverbs 12:18, I think before I speak and choose to speak truth in a loving way and not to tear anyone down.

Because I have faith that if I practice Mark 11:23 and Proverbs 18:21, I can manifest positive things over my life, and they will happen.

Yes, scripture has historically been used to tear someone like me down and I almost allowed it to happen. I just made the choice to use it to uplift others while encouraging myself in the process. I would hope others who share a similar narrative would do the same.

Dr. Christy Dinkins (she/her/hers)

A Queer Christian

Notes

[1]Victor H. Matthews and James C. Moyer, *The Old Testament: Text and Context*, 3rd ed. (Grand Rapids, MI: Baker Academic, 2012), 45.

[2]Hermann Gunnel, *Genesis: Translated and Interpreted by Hermann Gunkel*, trans. Mark E. Biddle (Macon, GA: Mercury University Press, 1997), 207.

[3]Colby Martin, *UnClobber: Rethinking Our Misuse of the Bible on Homosexuality* (Louisville, KY: Westminster John Knox Press, 2016), 58.

Chapter 3

The Sacredness of Dignity

"You shall not lie with a male as with a woman; it is an abomination."
—Leviticus 18:22

Since the author of Leviticus got to include several chapters about sex, it's only fitting that we get one, too. I mean, who doesn't like to mix Bible stories into their pillow talk? Anyone? Just me? All right then—I guess that solidifies my reputation as a nerd.

In all seriousness, this chapter is going to mention sex, ancient interpretations of gender roles, and the harm of patriarchal societies. Consider yourself warned and brace yourself accordingly.

Before we get to the sex talk, I'm going to take a minute to talk nerdy to you (see what I did there? "Nerdy" rhymes with "dirty," like the song "Talk Dirty to Me." I can't resist a good pun). Specifically, I'm going to talk about the nerdiness that surrounds fantasy stories. As a proud nerd myself, I love the lessons that hide within fantasy stories. So, take a pen out of your pocket protector and push those horn-rimmed glasses up your nose (I just did myself); we're getting nerdy.

In many popular fantasy stories, authors, scriptwriters, and game curators alike have invited us to ponder what happens to our own souls when we harm someone else. J.R.R. Tolkien, your local Dungeons and Dragons dungeon master, and even a certain T.E.R.F.-who-must-not-be-named[1] all posit in their own unique ways that if you hurt someone else–especially if you do so for selfish gain–you also hurt yourself.

Take Sméagol in *The Lord of the Rings* for example. At the start of *The Return of the King*, we see him in a flashback to an earlier time, long before he encounters Frodo and Sam, or even Bilbo, long before anyone referred to him by his other name Gollum. In this flashback, he looks positively fit as a fiddle and full of life. He's on a fishing expedition with his best friend to celebrate his birthday. They are both all smiles and having fun until they find the Ring of Power. When Sméagol sees the Ring for the first time, it immediately captivates him. He decides that he must get the Ring by any means necessary. The Ring made him less friendly in just a few moments, but it wasn't until he killed his best friend shortly thereafter to get it that something irreparably changed within him. His soul fractured as he felt no guilt or shame in the murder of his best friend. All that mattered was the he got what he wanted.

After the murder, Sméagol—now called Gollum because of the raspy, animal-like cough he developed—was banished from his village. He lost his capacity to show compassion to others and himself. He lost a drastic amount of weight, as his obsession with The Ring distracted him from his rumbling stomach. His physical appearance changed so much that he was no longer recognizable as the light-hearted, hobbit-like creature he once was. He was now a creature so full of hate that he couldn't even provide himself with more than the bare essentials to survive. His soul had fractured—he couldn't care for himself, let alone anyone else.[2] So, what does this idea of soul fracturing have to do with the rules for sex listed in Leviticus 18 and 20? A lot. Quite a lot, actually. Especially once we recognize that these chapters aren't about sex.

At this point you may be thinking, "But Kali, every single verse in Chapter 18 tells us who a man can or can't have sex with. You even made that terrible sex-related pun at the beginning of this chapter to set us up to talk about sex. How can you say that Leviticus 18 and 20 (but especially 18) aren't about sex?" Great questions all around, questions that I've asked myself several times. Today, though, I'd kindly suggest that if we think these chapters are about sex, then we're putting the emphasis on the wrong part of each verse. We've missed the point altogether. So, buckle up and, in the paraphrased words of Bilbo Baggins from *The Hobbit*, let's go on an adventure.[3]

Let's start by looking at Leviticus 18: 6-23. Yes, each verse mentions mention sex and who not to have it with, but look at what else they all have in common with each other outside of that. Nearly all of them imply dishonor. That may seem small to the modern eye, but in this ancient time, honor was everything.

The ancient Hebrews and most, if not all, cultures of the Ancient Near East lived in an honor/shame culture. Everything a man—yes, specifically a man because of the patriarchal system they lived in—did either brought honor or shame to his family or tribe. Even in the previous chapter, Abraham and Lot showed hospitality to strangers because that was the honorable thing to do in their culture. The citizens of Sodom and Gomorrah did not show hospitality to the angels, which brought the citizens shame and, ultimately, their own demise.

Additionally, the Hebrew culture of the time was working on what it meant to be set apart from the other religious communities. They kept many of these cultural statutes concerning hospitality, but also developed "Holiness Codes," rules designating what made someone ritually clean or unclean—that is, fit or unfit to enter into the temple grounds to worship God. While there is absolutely a large emphasis on the literal, physical cleanliness of the person who touches someone else's blood or bodily fluids—that's likely why the priest and the Levite pass by the injured man in Luke 10:25-37—there is a lot to be said on the spiritual cleanliness of the person. Take the commandment "Thou shall not kill" for example. The person committing the murder is physically defiled by literally having someone's blood on their hands, but they are also spiritually defiled because they played the role of God and took someone else's life. They dishonored themselves, their family, and that man's family by taking that man's life.

The only verse in Leviticus 18 that discusses the actually physically defiling thing about a man having sex with a woman is verse 19, where it says, "You shall not approach a woman to uncover her nakedness while she is in her menstrual uncleanliness." I think the "how" behind the physical uncleanliness there is clear. I would argue that, assuming the other women mentioned in this chapter aren't on their periods, the physical cleanliness or lack thereof in the actions isn't what the authors are calling into question in those other verses. If that were the case, they would have mentioned something about the physically dirty nature of intercourse. Some of you might be saying, "But Kali, surely the writers are highlighting that having sex with family members is a sin." Let me remind you that, in this time, it was commonplace for men to marry their first cousins. Men were also required by law to marry their brother's wife if their brother died. Family relations meant little when it came to looking at who would make a suitable wife for a man. The only thing that really mattered was whether that woman was already connected to a man.

When we get to Leviticus 18:6-23, it's less about who a man can or can't have sex with, but instead more about who a man dishonors by having sex

---

A Word About Patriarchy

For better or worse, our spiritual ancestors existed in a patriarchal culture—a culture in which only men were considered citizens in society. Women were considered property and were treated as such. Even today, the remnants of patriarchal interpretations of scripture have continued to lead to wrongly justifying the mistreatment of women across the globe. I say all this to say that when I remind us to remember the context of the book of Leviticus, I don't do so lightly. I believe that in order to create a more just society, we have to be diligent about what honors men, women, and non-binary folks. For the purposes of finding what my colleague and friend Myron Randall calls "the truth trapped in the text," we have to entertain this reminder about contextual social norms.

with the specific types of women listed. Because this culture was steeped in patriarchy, a man having sex with a woman the list prohibits is a sin because he dishonors the other man.[4] How? By violating that man's woman. The instructive nature of these verses is about a man honoring his father, brother, uncle, son, and any other man in his life by leaving their ~~property~~ women alone. Some of the verses in Chapter 18 indicate that the man dishonors himself when he commits these acts; others indicate he dishonors the other husband or brother of the woman he slept with. But when we get to verse 22, something changes:

"You shall not lie with a male as with a woman; it is an abomination." Other translations say, it is "detestable."[5]

This is your reminder to unclench your jaw, relax your shoulders, and take a deep breath.

I promise we're going somewhere life-giving.

What exactly is the author calling detestable? Is it the actual act of sexual intercourse? If we were emphasizing the correct parts of the previous verses, then we already know that the answer to that question is no. In order to understand what in this verse is detestable, we have to make sure we don't gloss over this part: "as one lies with a woman."

In the culture of this text, what did it mean to lie with a woman?

If you were a man, it meant viewing her as a means through which you could continue your lineage, fulfill your carnal desires, or both. It meant buying her from her father and having your way with her. That doesn't always have to look as aggressive as rape, but it comes back to the same idea: women weren't men and therefore weren't worthy of the same honor, respect, and dignity as men were. Women weren't citizens; they were property. To treat a man the way you treat a woman was to treat that man as property. To view a man as anything less than a man was the ultimate dishonor. And, as depicted by the consequence list in Leviticus 20, the penalty for that level of dishonor was death.

"As one lies with a woman" isn't a commentary on the mechanics of gay sex; it's about one man treating another without honor, respect, and dignity.[6] That denial of dignity is detestable because, just like with Sméagol and the Ring of Power, you damage your own soul when you fail to honor the dignity of another person.

Thankfully, humanity has grown over the millennia. Here in the United States, women are no longer considered property. We are considered full citizens under the law with the agency to live our lives as we see fit. We still don't make the same wages as our male counterparts for the same work as of the writing of this book, so there's definitely still room for improvement. Because our culture no longer matches the culture of the text, our application of the lessons in this text must shift.

Since women and female-bodied folks are finally considered people and not property, I believe we can responsibly apply the lesson of the text to all genders. And the lesson of the text is this: Do not violate the dignity of another person, for that is detestable. When you harm another person, you fracture your own soul because you hurt the image of God, which resides both in you and in the person you dishonor.

How does this translate to our daily lives? I'm confident that those of you reading this book and I are on the same page that forcing someone to have sex is inarguably bad, so how do we apply this lesson outside of the bedroom?

Every day, we are presented with countless opportunities to interact with people, be it our family, the cashier at the grocery store, or the panhandler at the off-ramp. Each of those encounters is an opportunity to treat another fellow human with dignity. A smile, a wave, a hug, a bottle of water and a $5 are small acts of everyday honor we can all easily incorporate into the rhythm of our lives. When we miss these opportunities or lash out in frustration at those before us, we run the risk of dishonoring both ourselves as well as those we engage in those moments. Our change might not be as dramatic or quick as Sméagol's transformation into Gollum, but those moments chip away at our souls, slowly stealing our joy, peace, and compassion until one day we wake up and realize that have become a modern-day Ebenezer Scrooge: bitter, hollow, and without compassion for our fellow humanity.

And that's the lesson here: Treat others with honor. Every person you encounter is a child of God, a divine creation worthy to be treated with dignity. When you honor them, you also honor yourself. How? Because when you treat someone with honor, you are embodying honorability yourself. You are how you treat people—nothing more, nothing less.

As you read these verses with fresh eyes, I want to encourage you to take a moment to sit with these truths. Paradigm shifts such as these take time to settle, and you owe it to you and your spiritual health to take that time. Use the questions below as a guide to help find your footing in this new interpretation. I hope you find healing in these reflections.

Reflection Questions

- How does shifting the emphasis from sex to honor and shame change how you read Leviticus 18 and 20?

- What does it mean to treat someone with honor? Is there ever a time when it's appropriate to treat someone dishonorably?

- Think of a time you dishonored someone (maybe a cashier or a customer service representative). How did you feel afterward?

- Think of a time you treated someone with dignity. How did it affect them? How did it affect you?

- Think of a time someone treated you dishonorably. How did it affect you? How did it change the person you were interacting with?

Prayer

Lord of all creation, of every person of every nation, grow in us an honorable spirit. Let us see your image in every person we encounter. Give us the strength to treat them with the honor and dignity you've already deemed them worthy to receive. And in the same vein, remind us that we are worthy of the same treatment because we, too, are children made in your image. Amen.

Interlude: Redemption and Renewal

For decades I fought it alone, consumed by a tormenting cycle: feminine expression, secrecy, regret, shame, sincere repentance, promises to God, and begging God to help me. The cycle always repeated, but divine help never came.

Paralleling this was an increasing addictive dependence on alcohol, risky behavior, and then secrecy and dishonesty to mask it all.

All because I misunderstood scripture. I misunderstood its purpose. I misunderstood its meaning. I misunderstood its methods. The divine help that never seemed to come was actually there all along. That's how God works. God is always present. God is always available. God always loves me. Nothing I can ever do will stop God from loving me!

The way that I was reading scripture was actually blocking me from my own soul, and obstructing my soul's relationship with God. Although I believed in the creative power of God, I limited that creativity to the first seven days of the world's existence, to the first few chapters of scripture. Creation for me was a starting point of the world, and provided exact molds into which each of us should fit. I tried to be what I was not, and not to be who I was, because I couldn't fit myself into any of the molds. The molds were not created by God—I constructed them.

God is creative. God is self-revealing. Why should I limit these traits of God to actions in the first few days of creation, or the first couple of centuries of decisions by the church? The wonderful discovery is that God created me uniquely. I was never meant to be Adam or Eve, or Abraham, or even Jesus. God meant for me to be who I am, and to spend my life discovering identity.

Jesus described himself as the way, the truth, and the life. I accept his self-description. He said that the most important things for me are to love God, others and myself. I affirm that calling. Together, these give us a comprehensive description of the core of God's identity, and the means by which to understand everything in scripture. That understanding completely changed my understanding of myself.

The questions for me in all of Scripture, and specifically in understanding my identity and orientation are:

On what path do I sense God leading me?

To whom does God ask me to be true?

What is the unique mold God has designed for my life?

Who has God told me to love?

Who has God told me not to love?

Is my love for God, for others, and for myself matching?

The answers to these questions invite me to a fuller understanding of God, of myself, of others, and of all creation. Grace and love release me from guilt and shame. Being myself, with my unique identity and orientation, enables me to know God.

Rev. Teri King, DMin (she/her)
A Transgender Christian, Recovering Addict (alcohol);
Mental Health Patient;
Lover of All

Notes

[1] T.E.R.F. is an acronym in pop-culture that stands for trans-exclusionary radical feminist.

[2] *The Lord of the Rings: The Return of the King*, directed by Peter Jackson (Burbank, CA: New Line Cinema, 2003), DVD.

[3] *The Hobbit: An Unexpected Journey*, directed by Peter Jackson (Burbank, CA: Warner Bros. Pictures, 2012), DVD.

[4] James V. Brownson, *Bible, Gender, Sexuality: Reframing the Church's Debate on Same-Sex Relationships* (Grand Rapids, MI/Cambridge, UK: William B. Eerdmans Publishing Company, 2013), 209.

[5] For example, the New International Version, the Christian Standard Bible, the Holman Christian Standard Bible, and the New Living Translation.

[6] Matthew Vines, *God and the Gay Christian: The Biblical Case in Support of Same-Sex Relationships* (New York: Convergent Books, 2014), 89 and 93. See also, Brownson, Bible, Gender, Sexuality, 83.

Chapter 4

Don't Be Deceived

"A woman shall not wear a man's apparel, nor shall a man put on a woman's garment.
For whosoever does such things is abhorrent to the LORD your God."
—Deuteronomy 22:5

When I was in seminary, Matthew Vines from The Reformation Project came to a special chapel service to discuss his then-new book *God and the Gay Christian*. As someone who was privately working out my own queerness, I'd been reading his book in the safety of my bedroom and hiding it under my pillow when I wasn't home. I was captivated by his argument and his interpretation of scripture. So when he came to my seminary, I quietly walked with my classmates into the chapel and sat, trying to stifle my eagerness (read: desperation) to learn more about what the Bible actually said about being gay. The whole time, I hoped my classmates wouldn't suspect that I might be gay because I came to this specific event.

At the end of his presentation, Matthew said something along the lines of, "Oh, I almost forgot! I normally do this at the beginning of talks like these, but we'll do this now." He then asked us a series of questions and requested that we raise our hands for whichever scenario applied to us. "Who here is straight?" The majority of the hands in the room shot up. "Who here is gay?" A few hands rose timidly. "And who here is questioning?" A few hands poked up above the heads of the crowd. My hand stayed firmly in my lap for each question as my heart raced. I don't know how successful I was at keeping my face from blushing or my hands from sweating. Even though everyone in the room was focused on Matthew and his presentation, I felt like every spotlight in the auditorium was shining directly on me. When the chapel was over, I left hurriedly so as to not make myself available to questions. It felt like those spotlights followed me all the way out the door and back to my apartment; they didn't turn off until I'd shut my bedroom door and collapsed on the bed.

As much as I hated working through my queerness by myself, I felt like I had no choice but to hide in plain sight. I knew that so many ministry doors would close for me if I opened the door to my closet. At the time I felt called to be a missionary, and the denomination I wanted to work with after graduation clearly stated in its bylaws that it would not commission gay missionaries to serve. As someone who's always been passionate about missions, wrestling with that reality often kept me awake at night. Nevertheless, I wasn't sure how much longer I could suffocate in that tiny closet.

On top of that, I have never been a terribly feminine woman. Even as a kid, I never wanted to play dress up with dresses or skirts; give me jeans and a button up shirt any day. I remember having a huge argument with my mom in middle school about how a) I couldn't wear basketball shorts to school anymore because it wasn't "lady like" to do so and b) if I insisted on wearing shorts in public, I needed to start shaving my legs. Dress shopping for things like formal and band concerts was always such a pain because I could never find a dress that felt like me.

They were all too frilly, too revealing, too pink, too bright, too … much. But whenever I wore a dress—or even light makeup, for that matter—I got flooded with compliments from family, friends, teachers, everyone. When I got those compliments, I wasn't sure how to react. The flattery was nice, sure— Who doesn't like being told that they look nice?—but it felt like I was being complimented for being someone other than myself. As I've gotten older, I realize that it didn't just feel like I was being complimented for not being myself, I was being complimented for not being myself. I was being complimented for presenting my femininity in a way that was more acceptable to them, not praised for presenting my femininity in the ways that are authentic to who I am. Their praise was my reward for fitting in the box they wanted me to stay in. As my understanding of how God made me has grown, their box got too small.

As we dig into the potential lessons that Deuteronomy 22:5 holds for us, I know that this chapter may be most challenging for our trans, nonbinary, and gender non-conforming siblings. As someone who is still working out her gender identity—but still uses she/her pronouns—I also know that I can't speak for members of those specific communities. It is my hope, though, to learn and to continue learning so that I might be a good minister to you as you navigate a world that is too cruel to you for no other reason than the fact that you exist. So let's take a deep breath, remember that God loves us exactly as we are, and dig deep together in the hopes of finding spiritual growth and nourishment.

In order to understand this verse, we must first understand the context in which it's written. Deuteronomy is a complex book, so this may require a bit of unpacking. We'll do the brunt of that work in this chapter so we don't have to get as bogged down with the context in the next chapter, which is about another verse from Deuteronomy.

The literary setting of the book of Deuteronomy is made clear in the first chapters. It is the account of Moses toward the end of his life. He realizes that he will not be able to join the Israelites in The Promised Land, so he provides this new generation with instructions for how to live in community with one another once they get to there. Most of the rules Moses gives between 12:1-26:15 can be categorized by their relationship to the Ten Commandments. Most of the laws are inspired by one of the Ten Commandments, and are grouped based on which Commandment inspired them.[1] If they aren't related to one of the Ten Commandments, then they likely tie back to the Greatest Commandment, the *Shema* in Deuteronomy 6:4-5.[2] The remainder of the book focuses on the blessings that come with following these laws and the curses that come with ignoring them. Deuteronomy 22:5 is found in the middle of the section pertaining to the sixth commandment, "Thou shall not murder."

While Moses undoubtedly gave these instructions in his lifetime, they were not recorded immediately. They were passed down by oral tradition for generations. Most scholars agree that this speech started to be written down during King Josiah's reign (between 640-609 BCE).

Josiah's monarchy was concerned with reforming the community and getting the Israelites to follow the religious ordinances more closely. The neighboring kingdoms did not abide by the same laws, and some of the Israelites were wooed by their neighbors' practices. So, King Josiah was working to reform the community so that the nation would not experience the punishment described at the end of Deuteronomy. Some scholars believe that the writing of Deuteronomy even extended into the Babylonian Exile (around 586-538 BCE), in which case the book would have served as a reminder to the Israelites that they were receiving their due punishment for not listening to the laws God laid out, but would also serve as a beacon of hope. What was the hope? If they committed themselves to following God's way again, then they could be delivered from this Exile and return to The Promised Land.

Why does this contextual information matter? It highlights to us that there was a specific purpose for the book and allows us to examine the verses in light of that purpose. This context also reminds us that this book was put together with a specific agenda: Get the Israelites to follow the rules, particularly the Greatest Commandment and the Ten Commandments. That agenda can be summed up in two thoughts. Firstly, it's about defining the relationship between faith and love. Secondly, it's about defining our relationship to God—love the Lord your God—and to others—the Ten Commandments.[3]

Now that we've gotten that context established, let's get into the actual verse itself.

Chapter 22 starts with rules about what someone should do if they see their neighbor's livestock wandering off or in some kind of distress. A few verses later, we see rules for engaging with wildlife and restrictions about mixing things, like fabrics and seed. In the middle of those teachings involving nature, we see verse 5, "A woman shall not wear a man's apparel, nor shall a man put on a woman's garment; for whosoever does such things is abhorrent to the Lord your God."

It seems such a random instruction, especially since it is bookended by teachings concerning nature. It also seems to be such an out-of-place instruction when we consider the themes of the book. The rules about the animals make sense with the theme of relating to our neighbors; everything before verse 5 is about caring for your neighbor and all the animal stuff after verse 5 is about caring for God's creation—a way to show love to God. We can even tie those things back to the commandment about murder. If we see a neighbor's livestock wandering off and do nothing about it, that's less food for our neighbor's family and could potentially kill them by starvation as a result. If we fail to care for God's creation, we play a part in killing something God loves. We can rationalize those teachings in light of the sixth commandment, but verse 5 seems out of place. How does the way we dress relate to murder?

This verse has puzzled rabbis for centuries, so we are not alone in our puzzlement. Let me start by saying that there is a wide consensus among rabbinic scholars that this verse is not about crossdressing. Even among all of the debates, there is general agreement about three main arguments that could explain what the authors were trying to achieve by including this verse. First, some scholars argue that by "men's clothing" the authors meant "armor."[4] If we examine the verse from that standpoint, it could simply be about making sure men didn't shirk their wartime responsibilities by dressing as women and hiding when they were conscripted for battle.[5] It could also mean making sure women didn't rise above their station in this patriarchal society.[6] The second argument has to do with "not mixing things" in order to maintain purity standards.[7] As we see throughout the rest of Deuteronomy and elsewhere in the Hebrew Bible, the ancient Israelites were highly concerned with categorizing things and making sure to not mix the categories. Men and women had separate worship spaces in the temple. The women were relegated to the outer courts or gardens while the men actually got to go inside. So insisting that they keep their dress was a way to make sure that someone didn't go where they shouldn't in the temple. The final argument deals with making sure men couldn't sneak into all-female spaces or vice versa to commit adultery,[8] which makes sense when we consider the rules about adultery that follow in verses 13-30.

Ultimately, all of the arguments—be it from making sure men go to war to making sure no one cheats on their spouse—come down to the idea of deception. It is sinful to deceive your neighbor or attempt to deceive God.

Unfortunately, the idea of "deception" is not new to those in the transgender community. It is often a way to discredit trans folks and paint them in some sort of twisted, nefarious light. In the 34th season of the show Survivor, we saw the damage such an accusation can do. In a heated tribal council one night, contestant Jeff Varner tried to move a target off his back by talking about how deceitful other players could be. He went on about how some people could be extremely endearing, but be hiding a huge secret all the same. In order to "prove" his point, Jeff outed contestant Zeke Smith as a transgender man on national television, claiming that Zeke had deceived everyone there into thinking that Zeke was someone he wasn't. After the tribe members sharply ridiculed Jeff for his actions, the host invited Zeke to speak. Of everything he said, this was the line that captivated audiences with its poignant sentiment: "I didn't want to be known as 'the trans Survivor player.' I wanted to be known as 'Zeke the Survivor player.'" In other words, "I just wanted to be known as me." Thankfully, the tribe and the host unanimously decided to kick Jeff off the show immediately. There wasn't even a vote.[9]

Let me be abundantly clear: Transgender, nonbinary, and gender nonconforming people are not being deceptive when they embrace their transgender, nonbinary, or gender non-conforming identity. In fact, they are practicing the opposite of deception: authenticity. By dressing how they chose, transgender and nonbinary folk are honestly showcasing the outward expression of their inward selves. When we force transgender, nonbinary people, and gender

---

A Word About Coming Out

When you stay in the closet for whatever reason, you aren't being deceptive. We've all had to stay in the closet for one reason or another as a way to protect ourselves. It's also a different experience for each person in the LGBTQ+ community. Zeke Smith commented in an interview that after he had publicly and medically transitioned, he moved to a new place where the people he'd meet would only ever know him as a man so that he didn't have to be judged by those who knew him before his transition.[10] Coming out or, as Cody Sanders says, inviting people into the sacred space of our identity is a holy, serious thing.[11] It's a personal choice—no one should determine for you when or if you come out. That's a conversation between you and God. In the meantime, remember that you are not being deceptive by setting healthy boundaries to keep you safe.

---

non-conforming to hide, we are sinning. We are sinning by forcing them to cover up the beautiful person that God created. We are sinning by coercing them to lie to themselves and the world about who they are.

This lesson extends beyond the LGBTQIA+ community. The same is true every time we tell a boy that he can't play with a doll, a girl she can't play with a fire truck, a Black, Brown, or Indigenous person that their hair, dress, or accent is inappropriate for work. Anytime we force someone to change a core aspect of who they are for our own comfort, we are sinning.

Some of you may be thinking, "Kali, don't you think that calling it sin is taking it a bit far? Sure, it's not nice and pretty mean spirited. But sin? Don't you think that's a little harsh?"

Not at all. If you remember from the earlier conversation about the context of this verse, Deuteronomy 22:5 falls into the category of laws inspired by the sixth commandment: Thou shall not murder. The argument most related to the text would likely be related to not donning clothes to sneak your way into a place to cause someone else harm. In today's context, though, I think there's another lesson we can bring to this text. When we force someone to take on an identity that is not true to who they are—through clothes, dialect, deadnaming, and misgendering—we are murdering their God-given identity. We are murdering their actual identity in favor of a false identity we find more comfortable. We are harming the image of God in that person and, therefore, we are hurting God as a result. You can't love God and harm God's creation; that is abhorrent to God. I know that's likely not what the writers of the text were thinking when they wrote this text, but I believe it stands as a reminder to us that God's word is free to adapt as the world does. The Holy Spirit will move as she sees fit, regardless of whatever boxes we try to keep her in. When the world adapts, so does God.

What can we learn from this text? Ironically, I think this verse ultimately comes down to deception. Deception is the act of intentionally lying to others in order to get something you want, regardless of how it hurts your neighbor. It is the act of forcing others to accept something as truth when it is a lie—and that is something that LGBTQIA+ folks have been on the receiving end of for as long as we can remember. We know our truth. We know how God made us. God revealing to us the gifts of our sexual orientation or gender identity is a private conversation. It's not a conference call. Homophobic people and transphobic people—or anyone else, for that matter—were not invited to listen in, thank you very much.

But perhaps deception is also the act of lying to ourselves, that we think that we know better than someone else how God made them to be. In the same way that no one else was part of the prayer conversations I've had with God about my sexual orientation, my calling as a pastor, or any other aspect of my life, I have not been in on the conversations you've had with God about learning the deepest truths of who you are. I would be deceiving myself into believing that I'm as all-knowing as God is if I were to tell you that you are wrong about how you were fearfully and wonderfully made.

So, my siblings, do not deceive yourself into thinking that God approves of us forcing our neighbors into molds that make us comfortable. God will not take lightly to our presenting a lie as truth. As we will see in the next chapter, God will break our molds and our expectations again and again.

Reflection Questions

- What was your coming out experience like? How did it connect you to the Divine?

- Think of a time that you were deceived by someone. How did that impact you? How did it change your relationship with that person?

- Think of a time you deceived someone. What was your motivation? How did it change your relationship with that person?

- Is it possible to deceive God? Why do you think people try to deceive God?

- What is a truth about yourself that you struggle to embrace? What step can you take today to better love that part of yourself?

Prayer

Lord of all creation, of all people of all nations, grow in us a spirit of authenticity. Give us the courage to embrace ourselves in the beautiful, complex, diverse ways you made us, and give us the openness to embrace others in that same way. Let us not give in to fear and deception, but instead let us choose the courage to seek your truth with the sincerity of those who simply want to know you better. Amen

Interlude: Taking It Back

I grew up with amazing Baptist Bible-believing, church-leading parents. I remember my deacon father leading family Bible studies in the spirit of 2 Timothy 2:15. Ironically, I didn't need much encouragement to love the Bible. I was obsessed—the intrigue, the drama, the scandal—as well as the redemption, the radical love, and what reclamation looked like for those who were marginalized. Jesus' ministry addressed both the religious and the rebel.

Reclaiming scripture reading as a spiritual practice requires starting with the word itself. According to The Online Etymology Dictionary, the word reclamation has roots in Latin and Old French. It is the action of crying out against or protesting something (15th Century), calling someone back (1630s), or claiming as a possession something taken away (1787). Synonyms are recapture, repossess, retrieve.[12]

Thus, I reclaim scripture reading as a spiritual practice for me as my protest, my calling back to love, and my repossessing of power. The Bible is weaponized against the LGBTQ+ community, used to cause harm when taken literally or out of context. So, my reclamation is also me taking power away from the very religious folks whom Jesus spent the majority of his ministry attempting to call out of their sin and call into the kingdom.

I was one of the religious folks Jesus would have dragged for filth. I was one who shunned people based on my assessment of their sin. I was a hypocrite, and I could not reconcile my queerness with my faith. I was a worship leader, on the preaching track and being queer wasn't permissible, period.

I remember being sidelined in ministry after confessing my relationship with a woman. That relationship had fizzled harshly, and I only "told on myself" because I was experiencing domestic violence. I was so embarrassed, as I have always been a private person. To my horror, my pastor shared my situation with church leaders so that they could pray for me. I am unsure if they prayed, but I cannot forget the way they looked at me with contempt.

It's ironic that the church and its leaders often love the music and ministry of people who are secretly LGBTQ+ as long as we are in the closet. But Jesus brought freedom to us and we do not have to ascribe to such bigoted ignorance.

As a follower of Jesus and his way, I struggle with the Bible when I consider it in the light of my Blackness, queerness, and womanhood. I am growing to understand the error(s) of humans and their proclivity to abuse the scriptures for the sake of power. This knowledge, and the freedom brought by the breath of God, has led to a liberation I didn't know I needed. Whom the son set free is free indeed, and my liberation includes finding solace and strength in the scriptures. I've reclaimed my time and scripture reading as a spiritual practice because it draws me closer to God in ways that can't be explained.

Autem Clay (she/hers)
A Queer Christian

Notes

[1]Patrick D. Miller, *Deuteronomy*, Interpretation: A Bible Commentary for Teaching and Preaching, ed. Patrick D. Miller (Louisville, KY: Westminster John Knox Press, 1990), 15. Terence E. Fretheim, *The Pentateuch*, Interpreting Biblical Texts, ed. Gene M. Tucker (Nashville: Abingdon Press, 1996), 156-7.

[2]Miller, 14.

[3]Ibid., 15.

[4]Kathy Bladock, *Walking the Bridgeless Canyon: Repairing the Breach between the Church and the LGBT Community* (Reno, NV: Canyonwalker Press, 2014), 242. Austen Hartke, *Transforming: The Bible and the Lives of Transgender Christians* (Louisville, KY: Westminster John Knox Press, 2018), 61.

[5]Bladock, 242.

[6]Miguel A. de la Torre, *Liberating Sexuality: Justice between the Sheets* (St Louis, MO: Chalice Press, 2016), 161.

[7]Bladock, 242. de la Torre, 161.

[8]Bladock, 242.

[9]*Survivor*, season 34, episode 6, "What Happened on Exile, Stays on Exile," aired April 12, 2017, CBS.

[10]Zeke Smith, "'Survivor' Contestant Opens Up About Being Outed as Transgender (GuestColumn," *The Hollywood Reporter*, April 12, 2017, https://www.hollywoodreporter.com/tv/tv-news/survivor-zeke-smith-outed-as-transgender-guest-column-991514/ (accessed June 29, 2021).

[11]Cody J. Sanders, *A Brief Guide to Ministry with LGBTQIA Youth* (Louisville, KY: Westminster John Knox Press, 2017), 46-49.

[12]*Etymonline: Online Etymology Dictionary*, "Reclamation (noun)," https://www.etymonline.com/word/reclamation#:~:text=reclamation%20(n.),protest%22%20(see %20reclaim) (accessed June 1, 2021).

Chapter 5

A Beautiful Arc

"No one whose testicles are crushed or whose penis is cut off shall be admitted into the assembly of the LORD."—Deuteronomy 23:1

One of my all-time favorite childhood television shows was *Avatar: The Last Airbender*. The animation was beautiful, the story captivating, and the characters endearing. As a kid, there were few shows that I regularly carved out time to watch. This show was one of those few, since this was back in the day that if you missed a new episode, you'd have to wait for the rerun to air. Kids today will never understand the struggle. From episode to episode, I was never disappointed. The show's creators always successfully immersed me into the show and took me on all of the adventures the characters experienced together. I'm a waterbender, if anyone was curious.

I was pleasantly surprised to see its popularity resurge during the self-isolation brought on by the COVID-19 pandemic. Perhaps it was simply because we were all stuck at home, needed something to watch, and realized the whole series—as well as the sequel series—had just dropped on Netflix. It was the perfect opportunity for a new generation of fans to binge watch it and fall in love with it like I had. Whatever the reason for this show's second life, it's been fun to see my social media feed constantly filled with pictures of air bison and wisdom from Uncle Iroh. I also got the opportunity to introduce my wife to the show, as she never watched it as a kid. It is now one of her favorite shows of all time.

Both my wife and I love several things about the show, but we are both consistently blown away by the redemption arc of one character: Zuko, the banished crown prince of the Fire Nation (major spoilers ahead for anyone who hasn't seen the series). When the series begins, Zuko is an angsty teenager with one goal: to restore his honor so that his abusive father would welcome him home. Zuko is convinced the only way that he can return home a hero is to capture the Avatar, a being that has been missing for one hundred years. All of the adults in his life recognized that Zuko's father sent him on a fool's errand, but Zuko–so desperate for affection and approval—clung to that mission as his last thread of hope. In the first season, he's harsh, hot-tempered, and down right mean. He constantly lashes out at the people who try to help him, including his ever-patient uncle. Anyone who sees Zuko in the first season agrees that he was, well, quite a jerk.

As the series progresses, Zuko experiences some intense character development—which is fascinating because he wasn't the main character. He experiences several hardships that allow him to see the underbelly of what his nation has done to the surrounding nations throughout the Hundred Year War. He learns the true horrors of war and realizes how he's been complicit in harming so many innocent lives. Eventually, he realizes that his father is a terrible, abusive person and chooses to align himself with the Avatar—the person who the show initially set up to be his biggest rival—in order to stop his father's tyrannical reign. By the end of the series, Zuko redeems his honor not by capturing the Avatar, but by embracing justice. The series ends with Zuko accepting his place as the new Fire Lord and declaring an era of peace between the nations. He becomes one of the wisest rulers his nation ever had, and the Avatar became his closest friend.[1]

I love this redemption arc so much because the writers chose to do something more challenging with Zuko's character. It would have been extremely easy for them to decide that Zuko would be the Avatar's nemesis for the whole series, have predictable fights between the Avatar and Zuko at the end of each season, and ultimately have the Avatar defeat Zuko at the end of the series. So many children's shows are predictable in that way. Instead, they looked at Zuko's original character and recognized that he had major potential. They realize that Zuko could represent the potentially thousands of kids who would watch the show, thinking that they might be "bad" because of how their parents treat them, and the writers gave those kids hope. If Zuko can find love, friendship, and healing, so can they.

If we let the first snapshot of Zuko be the sum total of who Zuko is, we've missed the redemption arc entirely. We can't let our introduction to him in season one determine how we are supposed to see him the whole show. We have to zoom out and see Zuko's entire experience in order to get a fuller picture of who he is. The message isn't in the scene where we meet him in episode one; the message is in his whole story.

Sometimes, scripture is like Zuko's redemption arc. In order to get the full picture, we have to zoom out, to look at the arc of multiple verses in order to understand one verse more fully. If we focus on just one verse, we miss the larger message in the text.

This reality is especially the case when we examine a verse like Deuteronomy 23:1. Read in isolation, this verse is particularly jarring. In order to fully understand Deuteronomy 23:1, we have to consider all of the contextual information we discussed in the last chapter. We know that the book of Deuteronomy is the collection of instructions from Moses to the Israelites as they prepare to enter The Promised Land, and all of these instructions are anchored either in the Ten Commandments or the Greatest Commandment. This verse falls within the chunk of passages that are supposedly inspired by the seventh commandment: Thou shall not commit adultery.[2]

So if these verses are supposed to connect to adultery, why are all of the instructions in verses 1-8 concerned with who's allowed to come into the assembly of the Lord?

If we think back to the Holiness Codes we briefly looked at in Chapter 3, I think we'll find some answers. Remember, the Ancient Israelites were extremely concerned with what made someone ritually clean or unclean. If someone was ritually unclean, they were not allowed into the temple for fear of defiling holy ground. In some cases, they weren't even allowed in the community at large—like the lepers—for fear of contaminating other community members with their dirtiness. When it came to other things that contaminated someone to the point that they weren't welcome into the temple for worship, the Israelites believed that idolatry was a form of adultery. It broke a covenant that the Israelites had with God. It was, in their eyes, an adultery of the spirit.

Adultery—whether it was spiritual or physical—made someone unclean and, therefore, unfit for worship in the temple.

With that context in mind, let's take a look at the verses that follow to see what we might be missing: "No Ammonite or Moabite shall be admitted into the assembly of the LORD. Even to the tenth generation, none of their descendants shall be admitted to the assembly of the LORD, because they did not meet you with food and water on your journey out of Egypt, and because they hired against you Baalam son of Beor, from Pethor of Mesopotamia, to curse you" (Deut 23:3-4).

A Word About Cherry-Picking

By this point, you know that examining context is central to how I study scripture. Without understanding the context of a scripture, we can easily pull one verse out of context ("cherry-pick") and use it to manipulate a situation for our own gain. Verses like this and others have been used for centuries to unjustly oppress Black, Ingenious, and other People of Color on "biblical" grounds. This practice is sinful because it harms people whom God created. As you continue your own study of scripture, I encourage you to continually examine the context so that you don't miss the central lesson of the text.

These verses say that no Ammonite or Moabite is to be admitted into the assembly of the Lord, likely because they worshiped other deities and were, in the Israelites' eyes, committing an adultery of the spirit. If that's the case—if their exclusion is set in stone—what happens when we zoom out to later parts of the Hebrew Bible? What do we do with Ruth? In the very beginning verses of the book of Ruth, we are told that she is a Moabite. By the end of the book, she marries an Israelite man. Was Boaz sinning by taking her as his wife? If he was in the wrong, then Ruth was in the wrong, too, according to Deuteronomy 23:3-4. But if Ruth and Boaz are in the wrong by marrying each other, then why is Ruth mentioned in the lineage of Jesus?

You may be thinking, "Okay fine, Kali. God made one exception. But Ruth was just that: an exception. That doesn't mean we can just open the temple up to anyone, right?"

Let's keep reading in Deuteronomy 23: "You shall not abhor any of the Egyptians, because you were an alien residing in their land. The children of the third generation that are born to them may be admitted to the assembly of the LORD."

In those two sentences, the Egyptians go from "not allowed" to "allowed" into the temple. The prohibitions on Egyptians in the temple aren't a forever-long indictment. God says that they will eventually be welcomed in. Jesus and his family even took refuge in Egypt when he was a child, which can serve as a literary reference to Egypt's redemption in God's eyes. We see that pattern repeated with the Moabites and all the other groups of people listed in these verses.

In every case, all of the people who are excluded in this passage get included later on—their own redemption arc, if you will.

In order to see the redemption arc for the eunuchs, transgender scholar Austen Hartke suggests that we have to zoom out from this chapter and Deuteronomy altogether, all the way to Isaiah 56.[3] That might seem like a large jump when we look at the page numbers in our Bibles, but when we consider the composition dates, it's not as large a jump as you would think.

Isaiah 56 was written during the Babylonian Exile, likely not much later than when Deuteronomy was finished. If you remember from the previous chapter, the Babylonian Exile was a time when the Israelites were trying to get back into God's favor so they could return to The Promised Land. As they are working on going back to The Promised Land, there are new challenges that they have to consider particularly concerning what made someone ritually fit for worship in the temple. They look to God for answers, and God provides additional commentary on the rules they had been operating by prior to the

Exile. When we get to Isaiah 56:3-5, God says this: "Do not let the foreigner joined to the LORD say, 'The LORD will surely separate me from his people'; and do not let the eunuch say, 'I am just a dry tree.' For thus says the LORD: To the eunuchs who keep my sabbaths, who choose the things that please me and hold fast my covenant, I will give, in my house and within my walls, a monument and a name better than sons and daughters; I will give them an everlasting name that shall not be cut off."

So here's the million dollar question: did God change God's mind? That question typically makes Christians uncomfortable because they believe that God is constant, never-changing. But Deuteronomy 23:1 clearly says that eunuchs are not allowed in the assembly of the Lord, and Isaiah 56 clearly says that God will bless the eunuchs who keep God's ways and give them a special place within the temple. So what other conclusion are we supposed to draw here?

I don't believe that God changed their mind. I think God offered a correction on something humanity messed up.

The Bible is full of times when the Divine offers a correction to humanity's misinterpretation of scripture, and I can think of no better example than Jesus' Sermon on the Mount. Throughout his discourse in Matthew 5, Jesus teaches those gathered about the complexities of Torah law. As he teaches, he begins his commentary on specific laws with "You have heard it said …" and concludes them with "But I say unto you …" Some evangelical pastors have argued that Jesus was abolishing the old laws, but that's not what he was doing at all. Jesus was a devout Jewish man who had spent his life studying to become a rabbi. He didn't come to change the laws, but to correct our understanding of them. He wasn't abolishing them; he was clarifying them.

In Isaiah 56, God offers a Sermon on the Mount style correction to Deuteronomy 23:1—a huge one. It could have read, "You have heard it said, 'No one whose testicles are crushed or whose penis is cut off shall be admitted to the assembly of the Lord,' but I say unto you, 'To the eunuchs who keep my sabbaths, who choose the things that please me and hold fast my covenant, I will give, in my house and within my walls, a monument and a name better than children; I will give them an everlasting name that shall not be cut off."

God may well have said, "You have heard it said, 'Keep the eunuchs out of the temple,' but I say unto you, 'They will have an honored seat in my own sanctuary.'"

The lesson: Scripture doesn't exist in a vacuum. It grows as our understanding of the Divine grows. It adapts with society even within its own pages. In order to learn from scripture, we have to be willing to adapt along with it.

Just like a good redemption arc, we have to zoom out to see the bigger picture. As we zoom out, we have to be willing to let God correct our perspective and listen for the "but I say unto you" moments.

That lesson might sound fine and good, but what about when it comes to our own personal spiritual growth? How can we apply this verse to our daily lives? For me, it's all about inclusion and embrace. People may have tried to exclude you based on who you are, how you look, the fact that you don't fit into their molds. But God says that you, beloved, are welcomed into the Kindom of God just as you are, and God has given you a gift greater than a legacy, an everlasting name that shall not be cut off. And that is a blessing no one can take that away from you.

Reflection Questions

- Think of one of your favorite television shows, books, or movies. Which character has the best redemption arc? How does that character's arc relate to the ways you've experienced redemption in your own life?

- How does reading Deuteronomy 23:1 in conjunction with Isaiah 56:3-5 affect your reading of both passages?

- What are some of the "but I say unto you" moments God's spoken into your life?

- What does it mean to "choose things that please" God?

- Think about a time when you felt truly embraced by a person or community. What about that moment felt holy?

Prayer

Lord of all creation, of every person of every nation, grow in us a humble spirit. Let us be ever open to the "but I say unto you" moments you present us throughout our lives and give us the courage to change our lives accordingly. Help us to see the redemption arcs not only in your holy scripture, but also in the holiness of our lives. Speak, Lord. We are listening. Amen.

Interlude: No Shame

For the community that I grew up in, scripture was used to force people to conform to the expectations of the community. Scripture was also used to preach hate toward those the community deemed "other"—whether they be Hispanics, Muslims, queer folks, or even women in leadership. This manipulation cultivated a culture of judgment, hate, and shame.

I first realized that I am gay somewhere between middle school and high school. Having grown up in the community that I did, I'd heard countless teachings against people who are gay. Realizing that I am gay opened up a world of self-hatred and shame. I had always been a shy kid, but upon this realization, I started to retreat further into myself to hide who I was. I put up walls so people wouldn't suspect.

I was ashamed to be who I am. I was ashamed because the community I grew up in told me that I was condemned just by being me.

I prayed to be straight. I wanted to "fit" into my family and into the church community. I continued to pray.

While the community around me preached judgment and shame, I studied scripture. And I began to see a different message from scripture.

Not one of judgment. But one of love, acceptance, and welcoming.

This was so counter to the Christianity I had grown up in, but it fit in more with the message of the Gospels. My life began to change when I realized that the true message of Christianity had nothing to do with hate and judgment. It all came down to love.

Jesus taught love and compassion. He ate with people who the culture at the time deemed outcasts and sinners. Jesus opened his arms to those who were on the outside of society. He welcomed those that his society deemed "other." If Jesus did not condemn the "other," why should the Christian Church do so? The answer is it shouldn't—it's antichrist.

When I came out in 2016, I wasn't surprised by the anger and visceral reactions directed at me by the community who had raised me—I had heard them go on countless tirades against LGBTQ+ for so many years at that point that I suspected what would happen when I came out. While it did not surprise me, I was disappointed and hurt. Disappointed that they couldn't see that God's love was for everyone with no disclaimers or exceptions. Hurt that they could not see that I am the same person I had always been. Disappointed that the community who raised me distorted the teachings of Jesus into one of judgment and intolerance. Hurt that they chose to disown me rather than wrestle with the possibility that they were wrong. They held tight to their fundamentalist beliefs out of fear. They embraced the adage of "love the sinner, hate the sin," which is nothing more than permission to judge and hate those that they deem as "other."

For more than a decade, I've been processing the emotional and psychological abuse of the theology I was taught as a child. Processing the shame and self-hatred that came from the words of fear, hate, and judgment that perpetuated throughout that community has not been an easy road.

It's an ongoing process to shed the shame, but it's a process worth taking. For there is love and acceptance and dignity in the process.

Hate tries, but love wins.

Haley M. Cawthon-Freels, MDiv (she/her)
A Gay Exvangelical Christ Follower

Notes

[1] *Avatar: The Last Airbender*, created by Michael Dante DiMartino and Bryan Konietzko, Nickelodeon Animation Studios, 2004-2008, *Neflix*, https://www.netflix.com/title/70142405.

[2] Patrick D. Miller, *Deuteronomy*, Interpretation: A Bible Commentary for Teaching and Preaching, edited by Patrick D. Miller (Louisville, KY: Westminster John Knox Press, 1990), 160.

[3] Austen Hartke, *Transforming: The Bible and the Lives of Transgender Christians* (Louisville, KY: Westminster John Knox Press, 2018), 89-98.

Chapter 6

Divine Certainty, Holy Mystery

"I praise you, for I am fearfully and wonderfully made. Wonderful are your works; that
I know full well."—Psalm 139:14

As a college student, I spent my summers working at a camp in the heart of the Smoky Mountains. It was beautiful. The place we affectionately nicknamed the 700 Acre Wood was full of surprises: creeks, rivers, crawfish, deer, a waterfall, more species of trees than you could count, and the most gorgeous sunsets you've ever seen. Every day there were new surprises to uncover in this wooded sanctuary. It was one of the greatest jobs I've ever had—I got paid to explore nature with kids! As I led kids on hikes, encouraged them on high-ropes courses, and played with them in the river, I was continually astounded by how beautiful everything surrounding us was. How did we luck out to spend the summer in a place like that?

That kind of beauty is all around is, and that beauty is incredibly diverse. Where God could have simply made one kind of tree, God made hundreds of species on the North American continent alone. Birds? Thousands of species. Bugs? About 10 quintillion individual bugs are alive on earth at any given time (that's a 10 followed by 16 zeros),[1] and all of them are distinct. From soil types to butterfly coloration to cloud appearance, the wonders of creation are endless. While there are many things we do know about the earth, there are innumerable things we still don't know. Scientists are daily making new discoveries about all kinds of things in nature. The place that most animal scientists agree still contains the most unknown wonders to us is the depths of the ocean.

While there's still so much to discover about the oceans, there is a lot of stuff we've learned about the fish that live there. Scientists estimate that there are 33,600 different species of fish throughout the world—and that's just the species we've discovered! Of those 33,600 fish species, between 450 and 500 (close to 15 percent) of them change gender throughout their lives.[2] Some fish—like the damsel fish—change from female to male when a certain environmental need arises.[3] Other fish—like the black sea bass and the kobudai—change gender from female to male when they reach a certain age as part of their normal life cycle. Still other fish—like the mangrove rivulus—are hermaphrodites. Some hermaphroditic fish keep both sex organs and are able to self-fertilize, while others eventually choose a gender based on what other the fish of their school do.

These discoveries puzzled scientists for decades, but a recent study revealed how the fish transition. The DNA of the fish doesn't change, but certain genes are "turned off," which requires the body to create new pathways for the DNA to replicate. Essentially, the fish rewire themselves on a molecular level without changing the core components of what makes them the fish they are. It's really a fascinating thing, a fact that makes me marvel at God's creativity in creation all the more.[4]

So, we know how the fish change genders, but scientists will never be able to get to the crux of why. Yes, we saw above that there may be certain environmental factors or life-cycle cues that lead to the change, but we don't know why that's the way things are for these fish. Why are they built that way?

It's a holy mystery.

As we dig into Psalm 139, we will quickly find that this psalm celebrates the marvelous design of creation; we'll see a lot of the creation themes we saw in Genesis 1 about God's sovereignty in their creative design. While that may seem like an obvious thing for a creation psalm to do, I think we'll also discover a few holy surprises along the way.

Psalm 139 is one of a handful of psalms that fall into the minor category of individual hymn of thanksgiving,[5] but has elements of a creation psalm as well. While ultimately a creation psalm, its thanksgiving psalm characteristics mean that it is intended to be a piece that elevates the sovereignty of God; who else could have created all of creation so masterfully? The two categories intertwine to make something beautifully thoughtful.

The narrative of this poem is told through the experience of one person—potentially David—marveling at God's creative expertise. While other creation psalms describe the wonder-filled beauty of the things in nature—plants, rivers, mountains, stars, and so on—all around us, this psalm specifically looks to the wonder of the psalmist's own humanity. "I praise you, for I am fearfully and wonderfully made. Wonderful are your works; that I know full well."

Anytime I've heard this passage taught, it was inevitably in a message about the beauty and creative functionality of God's physical designs. I have vivid memories of a series we did in my youth group about how many nerve endings we have in our eyes, how many times our veins would wrap around the earth if they were laid out flat, and other interesting trivia facts about how the human body is put together. My youth pastor—and so many other pastors, youth leaders, and other folks after my youth group days that I've lost count—would then go on to explain that this passage proves beyond a shadow of a doubt that God is real and that our physical bodies give us the proof we need to not question God's existence. They would always preach that part with such certainty—the physical nature of our bodies was the reality that connected us to the Divine the most.

While there's nothing wrong with encouraging students to find confirmation of God's existence in the beauty of their physical bodies, I think those leaders missed a major point—or two, actually. Firstly, this psalm isn't about certainty—it's about mystery. The psalmist is in awe not because he's certain of how God made him, but precisely because he's uncertain of how God made him and the rest of humanity. Even though we know that God forms us in our parent's womb, we don't know exactly how—and neither does anyone else. Verse 15 says that "my frame was not hidden from you, when I was being made in secret, intricately woven in the depths of the earth." Only God knows with certainty how we get put together; no one else was in the depths of the earth with us while God was weaving us together. We don't know what goes into the building of a body; we just know that one gets made.

The mystery in this text doesn't stop there. As we examine this verse more thoroughly, I think we'll notice something surprising, that second thing those leaders missed. There's nothing here to suggest that the psalmist is wondering about what makes his physical body. In each verse, the psalmist is talking about his thoughts, behaviors, even the words on his tongue. "O LORD, you have searched me and known me. You know when I sit down and when I rise up; you discern my thoughts from far away." The psalmist continues throughout verses 3-12 discussing behaviors of his that God knows.

> **A Word About Our Bodies**
>
> When we focus on the spiritual side of anything, I think we can quickly try to separate our body from our spirit, as if our spiritual experiences are only spiritual or our physical experiences are only physical. Even though the emphasis of this passage is on your the workings of your innermost parts, your physical body is full of wonder, too. Take a moment to notice your body. Have you loved it today? How has your body supported you today? Take a moment to love on God's creation (ie. YOU) a little today. Your body deserves it, and so do you.

When we get to verse 13, he says that God "formed my inward parts." This isn't a reference to the literal organs, but to the reality that the Ancient Israelites believed that their decision making and emotions came from their stomachs. They viewed the inward components as the things that determine someone's personality. In other words, the psalmist isn't marveling at how God made his body; he's bewildered by how God made his spirit. If we don't know exactly what goes into the building of a body, then we certainly don't know what goes into the construction of a spirit.

If this psalm is describing the mystery surrounding how God creates our souls, why do we teach this passage as a commentary on the certainty of how God created the human body? Even to go back to the example of the fish I used in the introduction of this chapter, we aren't certain why those fish change and adapt the way that they do. If we can't be certain about something as simple as a fish, how can we fool ourselves into thinking we can claim certainty about something as complex as a human body?

Why do we proclaim false certainty about something so mysterious?

Perhaps it's a veiled attempt to convince ourselves that we have any control over God's creative design.

In tension with everything I've said thus far, it's also important to highlight that there is certainty in Psalm 139—it's just not where we've been taught that it is. All of the certainty in this passage is had by God, not the psalmist. In every verse, the psalmist is talking about all the things that God knows, not the things the writer himself knows. In verse 8, the psalmist goes so far as to say, "Such knowledge is too wonderful for me; it is so high that I cannot attain it." In other words, "There's no way for me to know all the things that God knows, even about my own self."

For us to use this passage as a claim to biological or spiritual certainty is heresy.

I want to be clear here: For you to claim certainty about how God is guiding your journey of self-discovery is good and right. There are core truths about ourselves that we've known our whole lives. For me, one of those truths I realized early on is I can't stand it when someone gets left out. Other, more complicated truths about myself are things God has revealed to me over the years of prayer, discernment, and living I've done on this earth.

As God reveals to you truths about yourself, you should feel the freedom to hold those truths with confidence. Those revelations are divine gifts—gifts crafted especially for you by the Divine themselves—and you should cherish them. What is heresy is for me to claim certainty about how God created you, especially if we've never met. Like me, you were "made in secret, intricately woven in the depths of the earth." No one knows what makes up the core components of who you are except for God and you as God reveals those things to you. This passage has been used incorrectly to claim certainty over the lives and bodies of LGBTQIA+ folks by people who have no claim to that certainty.

The only certainty this passage talks about is the certainty God has when it comes to how God created each of us. What is divine certainty to God is simply holy mystery to us. Every day is a new discovery of holy surprises that God put in our bodies and in our spirits.

God knows everything about us even though we are mysteries. We have microscopic spiritual galaxies contained within our flesh, and that is something that will never cease to amaze me. You are full of majesty and mystery, levity and depth, love and grace. All of those things are far too complex, far too terrifying to make sense of on our own; perhaps that's why the psalmist tells God that he knows that he is "fearfully and wonderfully made." As we engage with the Divine to learn more about the galaxies we contain, we constantly learn more about ourselves. We uncover some of the holy surprises God left for us to discover.

That's the lesson hidden in this text. Psalm 139 isn't about the certainty of God's creation, but about the never-ending mystery of it. You can examine your innermost parts your entire life and never go beyond the tip of the iceberg of things that God has put within you. May you feel the freedom to explore, to discover the mysteries that God has hidden in the depths of your being. You are as vast as the ocean; there is still much for you to discover, beloved. Dive deep and keep exploring.

Reflection Questions

- What's the coolest thing you've found in creation? What was so special about it?

- Have there been times you thought you were certain about something and ended up surprised? What was the process of moving from "certainty" to holy surprise like?

- How does shifting the emphasis from "body" to "spirit" change how you read this passage?

- What is something about yourself you've known as long as you can remember? What about something that you only learned recently?

- What is it like to know that there are things about you that God hid within you, but you haven't discovered yet?

Prayer

Lord of all creation, of every people from every nation, grow in us a spirit of mystery. Let us remove false certainty from our lives and, instead, let us be open to the holy surprises you have in store for us. Give a spirit of openness, that we would be willing to trust the experiences of those different from us, trusting that you are guiding them on their journey of self-discovery. Remove from us the desire to "play God," and instead bless us with the understanding to see when you are revealing holy mysteries to us and to others. Let us not be blind to the wonder you've surrounded us with. Let us, instead, embrace the uncertainty with open arms. Amen.

Interlude: Wonder and Awe

Growing up, there was seemingly only one way acceptable to read the bible: literally.

The culture around, particularly in the South, uses scripture to reinforce norms such as heteronormativity, male superiority, and women taking roles in society that are seen as "less than." They quote scripture such as the verse in 1 Corinthians that tells women to be silent in church. They quote Leviticus to justify homophobia, particularly homophobia against gay men. There are these and many other verses that have been used to justify all sorts of ways that the church has excluded those it has deemed the "undesirable."

Scripture is important. It's important to read and meditate on the words inspired by the Divine. But it's important to read scripture in the context, time, and place that it was written for, but also a realization that books on a page do not tell the entire story. In the book of Genesis it is stated that God created the heavens and the Earth, the sea, the forests, mountains, and all sorts of creatures. But as we look around creation we realize that there is more to the earth than just what is named in that story. Did God not also create swamps, marshes, coral reefs, deserts, and glaciers? If creation is this big, why does creation have to be limited to just male and female?[6]

How I have reclaimed reading scripture is a realization that God is beyond any of our comprehension. All creatures and humans of all stripes are named by God and created in their image. Knowing that no human entity can adequately define God, I can simply stand in awe of what they have made here on Earth and what they have imbued into each and every person I meet. Whenever someone puts limits on God, they are not glorified. When I think of my own identity, a non-binary on the asexual spectrum, I rejoice for the wonder of who God has made me.

Will Root (he/they)
An Asexual, Nonbinary Christian

Notes

[1]"Number of Insects (Species and Individuals," *Smithsonian*, https://www.si.edu/spotlight/buginfo/bugnos (accessed May 15, 2021).

[2]Vic Lang'at Junior, "How Many Species of Fish Are There?," World Facts, *World Atlas*, January 10, 2019, https://www.worldatlas.com/articles/how-many-species-of-fish-are-there.html (accessed May 15, 2021).

[3]"9 Species of Fish that Change Gender (with Pictures)," *Wildlife Informer*, https://wildlifeinformer.com/fish-that-change-gender/ (accessed May 15, 2021).

[4]La Trobe University, "Secrets of a sex-changing fish revealed," *ScienceDaily*, July 10, 2019, https://www.sciencedaily.com/releases/2019/07/190710163416.htm (accessed May 15, 2021).

[5]Nancy deClaissé-Walford, *Introduction to the Psalms: A Song from Ancient Israel* (St Louis, MO: Chalice Press, 2004), 150.

[6]Austin Hartke, *Transforming: The Bible and the Lives of Transgender Christians* (Louisville, KY: Westminster John Knox Press, 2017), 51.

Chapter 7

The Weight of Authority

"For this reason God gave them up to degrading passions. Their women exchanged natural intercourse for unnatural, and in the same way also the men, giving up natural intercourse with women, were consumed with passion for one another."
—*Romans 1:26-27*

Like many people, my first job was in the service industry. The summer after I graduated high school, I put in several applications all over my small town and got no after no until a certain fast-food restaurant with golden arches gave me a yes. It certainly wasn't my first choice, but it was the one that gave me a shot. I remember getting ready for my first day of work, trying not to get my hopes up for an amazing experience. After all, I'd heard stories from classmates working in fast-food joints. Let's just say they weren't loving it.

To say I was shocked was an understatement. My store manager took great pride in not only making sure our customers were served quickly, but treated well. During the breakfast rush, we had to make a fresh pot of coffee every 12 minutes on the dot to make sure our guests got the freshest cup in town. During slow times, we waited until a customer came in to drop a basket of fries into the fryer so our guests wouldn't have cold, soggy ones for their snack. When families with kids came in, we were instructed to kneel down, look the kids in the eyes, and ask the kids directly for their order so that the kids felt valued and seen. My store manager constantly challenged us to go above and beyond in how we treated our customers.

Not only did he want to make sure the customers were treated well, he worked hard to make sure that we—his employees—were well-treated, too. If we needed more hours, all we had to do was ask. Family emergency? He was the first to send condolences (and to send any leftovers that we'd have to throw out anyway). When a customer called one of the shift managers a racist slur, he promptly kicked her and her whole family out and gave the shift manager an extra break. For students like me who would be going to college at the end of the summer, he made it abundantly clear that we were welcome to come work as much as we wanted during breaks. He invested in us, and encouraged us to use our talents to make the guests feel welcome. Even though it was just a fast-food joint, he wanted to make sure everyone in the building—guests, staff, and others—left having had a good experience. He made that experience so positive for me that I regularly tell people that this golden-arched restaurant was my first job and I absolutely loved it.

When I left for my first semester of college, I transferred to another restaurant in the same franchise in my college town. If my previous boss was the epitome of a good manager, my new boss—let's just say he left certain skills to be desired. He didn't care if the service times for the drive through window were high or that those waiting got impatient—even though we were the busiest store in the franchise. He was not against serving customers stale coffee so that we didn't have to make a fresh pot. We were never allowed to clock in even just five minutes early, no matter how busy the restaurant was at the time. When I tried to do some of the things I'd been trained to do at the other restaurant, I was told that it was a "waste of time" because "nobody cared." During that semester, I got hurt and had to be on crutches for several months. My boss refused to work with me to figure out a way for me to work. To be fair, having the crutches behind the counter would have been a safety concern for my fellow coworkers. Ultimately, I quit so I didn't have to deal with the shame of being fired. That was one of the worst work environments I've dealt with in my working career to this day.

In the context that Paul wrote this infamous letter to the church in Rome, another "bad manager" sat on the throne of Rome: Gaius Caligula. Caligula was as corrupt as one could get. He used his authority to advance his own wealth and greed. He regularly had lavish feasts at taxpayers' expense, crucified followers of Jesus—and lined the streets of Rome with those poor souls' mangled bodies—and took more wives and concubines than one could count. He could have given Solomon a run for his money. On top of that, he regularly raped his male servants who, according to historical customs of the time, would likely have been around the age of twelve. For Caligula, life was all pleasure all the time, at everyone else's expense.

Why bring all this up about Caligula? Because Paul does—sneakily.

Some scholars believe that in Chapter 1 of the book of Romans, Paul is indirectly referring to not just any people who twist the law for their own perverse desires, but specifically referring to the current occupant of the throne.[1] As a Roman citizen himself, Paul couldn't directly call Caligula out for his sinful behavior—lest Paul became one of the crucified bodies lining the streets—so he does it indirectly, all the while providing enough context for the church at Rome to know exactly who he is talking about. By doing it this way, Paul is able to provide the church at Rome a concrete example of what not to do with the law and provide a clear picture of why the Gospel of Jesus is a better "law" to follow.

When we get to verse 24 of Chapter 1, some scholars believe Paul is describing Caligula's reign and, in the verses that follow, what life in the palace was like at that time: "Therefore God gave them up in the lusts of their hearts to impurity, to the degrading of their bodies among themselves, because they exchanged the truth about God for a lie and worshiped and served the creature rather than the Creator ... For this reason, God gave them up to degrading passions."

Everyone in the palace had one job: satisfy Caligula's every desire. Be that with food, drink, entertainment, or sexual gratification, that was their job. Yes, even the women who "exchanged natural relations with unnatural ones" were providing Caligula with pleasure. If you know the statistics of what kind of porn straight people in the United States stream the most, this isn't surprising. Lesbian porn is the second-most searched genre.[2] As we discussed earlier, women in patriarchal societies like this didn't have the agency to say what could or could not be done to or with their bodies. This passage doesn't say this explicitly, but, knowing the context of the time, it wouldn't be a stretch to suggest that the women in the palace only did those acts to placate a tyrannical and unpredictably cruel emperor.

So, what does this history lesson have to do with us? I think it's safe to say that we don't have a full palace of servants at our command to order around as we please. Since that's the case, what lesson is trapped in the text and how can it aid our spiritual growth?

We've all been in places of authority or have been in situations where others had authority over us. We've all seen people who handle authority well, and we've seen people who don't.

People who handle authority well make the environment around them a positive place where growth can happen and happens abundantly. Good leaders challenge us to become better and enhance the atmosphere overall as a result.

Even if you don't see it in the more "traditional" sense, you still have authority. If you're a parent, you have authority over your children. If you're

> **A Word About Authority**
>
> I think when most people hear the word "authority," they think about "power," but not necessarily in the positive sense. They think of people who can get stuff done, no matter who it might hurt. I prefer to think of "authority" as "servant leadership" instead. Servant leaders know how to lead a team or family well, but are also skilled at highlighting the experience of everyone involved. Who has been the most impactful servant leader in your life?

in the service industry, you have authority over the quality of service your clients receive. If you have a beating heart, you have authority to deem yourself worthy of proper love and care. We all have authority, and we probably have authority in multiple places in our lives. Be it at work, at home, or in our own spirits, we all have authority in some capacity.

So, the lesson is this: treat your authority with care. In the wise words of Uncle Ben from the Spiderman franchise, "With great power comes great responsibility." I doubt many of us get to Caligula-level abuse of authority, but we are all tempted to use our authority for our own satisfaction.

No one is above this temptation, not even Jesus. Think back to Matthew 4, when Jesus was fasting in the desert and then tempted by the devil. In verses 1-11, the devil presents Jesus with three different temptations: make bread from the stones; risk his life so the angels would save him; worship the devil in order to gain authority over all of the kingdoms of the world.

These temptations may seem like three distinctly different challenges that Jesus had to overcome in the moment, but I think they have more in common than one might think. In each scenario, Jesus is tempted to exercise different aspects of his power. Not only that, he's tempted to use his power to manipulate these situations for his own personal gain. Had Jesus succumbed to the temptations, he would have taken actions that separated his experience from the experience of common humanity.

I imagine that Gaius Caligula was tempted in the same way. I can imagine the devil whispering in his ear as his stomach rumbled, "Hungry? Increase the taxes so you can fill your belly with the most delectable treats. Who cares if the peasants starve? You're the emperor. It's only fitting that you have the best." As he looked at neighboring territories and weighed the risk to his life it would be to conquer them, I imagine the devil whispered, "Do it anyway—your guards will save you. It's their job, so who cares if they die while doing it? That's what they're supposed to do." And as his vision expanded to see all the territories of the world, I imagine the devil whispering to him, "Let me teach you in the ways of manipulation and power, and all you see and more can be yours to control."

Caligula was tested the same way that Jesus was and Caligula failed—miserably. And countless people suffered as a result.

When we are similarly tempted, I believe the Greatest Commandment can be our anchor. If we're not sure if we should do the thing we're tempted to do, we can ask ourselves, "Will this help me healthily love me? Will it help me love my neighbor?" If the answer to both of those things is yes, then you can be pretty confident it will help you love God as a result. If the answer to either of those things is no, then that's a good indicator that you might be about to manipulate a situation for selfish gain.

I also want to be clear here: Showing love to yourself does not mean being selfish. Some may look at Caligula's life and claim that his problem was that he loved himself too much. On the contrary, I'd argue he didn't love himself at all. Loving yourself well includes holding yourself accountable for when you've messed up. Loving yourself requires owning up to the harm that you've caused your neighbor and committing to do better. Caligula did none of those things. He engaged in an idolatry of the self, which led to his self-worship at the expense of others. Had he loved himself with a real love that included real accountability, he would have been a better steward of his authority.

As co-creators made by the Creator, we all have the autonomy to decide how we treat others. We have the capacity to use our authority in ways that show love to ourselves, but not at the detriment of our neighbors. As you take these lessons with you, it is my fervent prayer that we strive to show the servant leadership Christ himself modeled for us with his very life. We might just find some fulfillment there.

Reflection Questions

- Think of the best boss you ever had. What made them so great to work for? What about your worst boss? What made working for them such a challenge?

- What areas in your life is your authority most evident? What places in your life do you have authority in a more subtle way?

- How can you be a better steward of your authority?

- How does viewing the Temptations of Jesus as a lesson on stewarding authority change your perspective of that story? How does it change how you read Romans 1?

Prayer

Lord of all Creation, of every person of every nation, grow in us a discerning spirit. Show us where we have authority and help us use it wisely. Let us be quick to see if an action would hurt ourselves and others, and quick to seek healing when we've caused harm. Teach us to be wise in the ways of Christ's servant leadership and grow in us the strength to live out those actions in our day-to-day lives, both for our sake and our neighbors'. Amen.

Interlude: On Divine Assignment

Scripture and prayer are my anchors and foundation. They help me recenter and reconnect directly to God, the Divine. Scripture humbles me. Reading scripture gives me transformative power, understanding, a change in perspective and, at times, a much needed change in direction. It serves as my raw truth, my teacher, my resource, and my GPS for life's circumstances. I hold it in great veneration because I seek to uphold Christ's teachings of loving God, my neighbor, as well as myself.

I am a transmasculine/transgender male. Intersectionally, I have experienced enmity from strangers in passing via racial and homophobic slurs as well as physically noticeable displays of discomfort and disgust. In no way have those encounters deterred me from living authentically, unapologetically, and unashamed. I understand that even though I am in the world, I do not have to be of it. Scripture reassures me that God's love is consistent even if that is not always reflected through my human experiences or circumstances. It has been during trials that I have found peace, comfort, reassurance, forgiveness, grace, restoration, and healing through reading and meditating on scripture. Even when I have strayed, I have been able to reclaim my identity in Christ by understanding that I am loved in spite of.

On the other side of the coin, I have encountered others with whom I have been embraced and wholeheartedly accepted. I believe that there is a significant and divine assignment for the LGBTQIA+ community and allies to serve as direct extensions and examples of Christ's unconditional love. Personally, I feel like I've been equipped to stand in the gap to serve as a connector to those that may have been overlooked, disrespected, viewed through the lens of inequality, or have been rejected or felt unloved as results of their experiences both inside and outside of the church. I find it necessary to serve as a pillar and support to remind them that are not excluded from being in relationship with God because they are a queer Christian. God has use of all, all are worthy, all are created from love, all are love, all can love others freely, and all deserve to be loved and respected.

Saavedra "Ve" Ivey (he/him)
A Transgender Christian

Notes

[1]James V. Brownson, *Bible, Gender, Sexuality: Reframing the Church's Debate on Same-Sex Relationships* (Grand Rapids, MI/Cambridge, UK: William B. Eerdmans Publishing Company, 2013), 156-161.

[2]Olga Khaza, "Why Straight Men Gaze at Gay Women: The Psychology Behind the Male Sexual Desire for Lesbians," *The Atlantic* (March 8, 2016), https://www.theatlantic.com/health/archive/2016/03/straight-men-and-lesbian-porn/472521/ (accessed on March 27, 2021).

Chapter 8

Matters of the Heart

"But now I am writing to you not to associate with anyone who bears the name of brother or sister who is sexually immoral or greedy, or is an idolater, reviler, drunkard, or robber. Do not even eat with such a one."—1 Corinthians 6:11

For whatever reason, our culture has long associated femininity with being "soft." By "soft," I mean "not strong," "delicate," or "fragile." That is to say for anyone—man, woman, non-binary person—to show softness in emotion, physicality, or otherwise is to indicate they aren't strong. We conclude that strong and soft have to be mutually exclusive ideas, polar opposites that can't exist in the same space—another shortfall of binary thinking.

But for all of that consensus, we ignore the evidence of our daily lived experiences. We forget that softness and strength can coexist within the same person, and often do. Think of all the parents you know who will go to any lengths to protect their children, and in the same breath can cradle their children in the most tender of embraces when that child starts crying about a nightmare they had. Perhaps this image is easier to imagine if we picture a feminine person in this role, but I believe softness and strength exist in each of us.

> **A Word About "Homosexuality"**
>
> In order to do this passage justice, I have to bend our rules of engagement to discuss the "h-word." This word didn't appear anywhere in English documents until the late 1800s and was not added to any English Bible until 1946. You read that right—this word has only been in the Bible for less time than Betty White has been alive. And I'm pretty sure she'd say its addition was not golden. The word in this passage that gets mistranslated as the "h-word" or "sexually immoral" would be better translated as "soft," as in "someone with weak morals."1 For a more in-depth word study, check out James Brownson's *Bible, Gender, and Sexuality*.

Take my friend and colleague Kristian Smith, Lead Pastor of The Faith Community where I also pastor. One of his many entrepreneurial enterprises is his business P-Squared Custom Clothiers. He takes great pride in being able to curate beautiful, sleek designs for both himself and his clients. Seriously, go to https://psquaredclothiers.com and check out his suits, shoes, and pocket squares. They are stunning. He also has pierced ears and models most of his own products on his business's social media platforms. Because he takes fashion and design so seriously, many people assume that he's gay because they attribute those qualities as feminine and, therefore, automatically queer for a man to have. They also point to his work as a radically phenomenal LGBTQIA+ ally in numerous Christian spaces and assume people can only be that invested in the work of inclusion if they are a part of the LGBTQIA+ community themselves.

But he's not gay. He's straight as an arrow and married to an equally phenomenal woman. He's also in the College Football Hall of Fame, an achievement I believe most people would say is incredibly masculine. Kristian is one of the strongest people I know physically, emotionally, and spiritually while simultaneously having soft spots for Black empowerment, LGBTQIA+ rights, women's rights, his family, and fashion. Within his personhood, softness and strength are not mutually exclusive, but tightly interwoven to create his identity. If you take one part away, he's no longer the Kristian God made.

You might be thinking, "Okay fine, Kali. We're allowed one exception to the rule. But there aren't biblical examples of strong men with soft hearts, right? God always condemns soft-hearted men because the Bible was written in patriarchal societies, right?" Let's take a look at some other scriptural narratives to find out.

Before we get to the lessons in 1 Corinthians 6:9-11, let's take one last look at the Hebrew Bible for some assistance. In Genesis Chapter 25, we see a tale of the two brothers Jacob and Esau, the sons of Isaac. Esau was the eldest and, as custom dictated, was to receive the greatest inheritance and blessing from his father whenever his father died. Esau was the one primarily responsible for continuing the family legacy. On top of that, he was burly, hairy, a great hunter—everything that his culture expected a good man to be. Jacob, the second-born, was smaller, smooth-skinned, and more often than not stayed home to help his mother in the kitchen. By all accounts, Jacob was a "soft" man—nothing close to the ideal "man's man" his culture expected. No reader of that time would be surprised by the fact that Esau was the one destined to continue the family legacy.

Fast forward to Genesis 27. Isaac is on his death-bed and prepares to bless both Esau and Jacob. Through an act of cunning, Jacob, not Esau, received the blessing of the first-born son from Isaac. And it doesn't stop at the blessing. Jacob is the one who wrestled with God on the banks of the river Jabok.

Jacob is the one whom God renamed Israel. Jacob is the one who fathered the 12 sons who would lead the 12 tribes of Israel. If Paul (a former Pharisee who knows the Hebrew Bible like the back of his hand) argues that being a "soft," effeminate man was sinful, why would God go out of God's way to bless Jacob? Why would God beget the nation of Israel from a "soft" man like Jacob instead of a "man's man" like Esau? Did Paul overlook this story in his studies to become a Pharisee?

I believe Paul would actually argue that Esau, not Jacob, was the "soft" man in this story.

Among other things, Esau willingly traded his inheritance for a bowl of soup because he was hungry; he was undisciplined. I believe Paul would argue that, while Esau was strong physically, Esau was weak in a very different way: he had weakness of the heart.

In English, we often use one word to describe many different things, which consistently leads to confusion. I think our past interpretations of this verse may be one of those times. When we get to 1 Corinthians, I believe we're using the same English word to describe two different concepts: "soft" as in "feminine" and "soft" as in "weak." What if in 1 Corinthians, Paul isn't describing femininity as a sin, but is instead describing weak-heartedness as a sin? That might not be as far a stretch as we might think.

If we look at the beginning of Chapter 6 in 1 Corinthians, we see that Paul is admonishing the church in Corinth because some of the members have started a slew of petty lawsuits. Instead of handling these issues within the church community, some members have taken to working with people outside the church—people unfamiliar with the moral and ethical standards unique to this community—to side with them and settle their disputes. Paul claims that by handling the disputes in this way, these members are shaming fellow believers in front of non-believers and overall weakening the standing of both the church in this city and the Gospel across the land.

Paul goes on to remind them that evil doers will not inherit the Kindom of God, giving examples of who he considers to be evil doers: sexually immoral people, adulterers, idolaters, and—using our corrected translation—weak-hearted people, thieves, greedy people, slanderers, and swindlers.

It's interesting how Paul labels people in this list. I can't think of many people who are those people 24/7, but I can think of several people who have had weak-hearted moments—myself included! But what does it mean to have a weak-hearted moment? For me, a weak-hearted moment is a moment when you give into the temptation to do something that is against your moral code. Depending on your moral code, that can look different for everyone.

Maybe it looks like lying to your partner about a credit card charge when you are adamantly against lying. Maybe it looks like lashing out in anger instead of asking your friend why they did a certain thing that bothered you. The list could go on and on since weak-hearted moments look different for each of us.

The Bible is chockfull of examples of people with extreme weak-hearted moments: David when he committed adultery with Bathsheba and had her husband murdered; Judas when he sold Jesus out for 30 pieces of silver; Peter when he denied Jesus three times. The list could go on and on. All of these men showed weak-heartedness for a moment of pleasure or social gain. Even Paul had his weak-hearted moments, as a former persecutor of the early followers of Jesus himself. He was famous for holding the coats of the men who stoned the apostle Stephen to death because of Stephen's faith in Jesus.

But as angry as Paul is with the citizens of Corinth for their petty squabbles, he still takes the time to remind them of God's grace. He said that some of them had, indeed, been the people he listed in his evil-doer list and then reminded them, "But you were washed, you were sanctified in the name of the Lord Jesus Christ and by the Spirit of our God."

Thank God for Jesus.

Because of Jesus, we aren't defined by our weak-hearted moments. We are instead defined by our ability to seek forgiveness and live into our God-given identities. Peter became one of the most important figures of the early church. Paul became one of the greatest apostles of all time. David was one whom God called "beloved." Judas—well, he never sought forgiveness for his trespasses. And perhaps that indicates that one of the largest pitfalls of weak-hearted moments is stubbornness and a refusal to admit when we've hurt our neighbor. I have every confidence that, had Judas repented of his sin and asked Jesus' forgiveness, Jesus would have welcomed him with open arms. Let us not forget that at the Last Supper, Jesus fed Judas, too. I firmly believe grace was waiting for Judas.

That grace doesn't just show up in the Christian Testament. Let's jump back to Genesis one last time. In Genesis 33, Jacob returns to the land of his father and encounters his brother Esau on the way. Jacob was nervous about the encounter and was preparing to woo his brother with gifts in order to try to stave off any potential conflict. He assumed Esau was still angry about Jacob stealing the blessing and inheritance. As they approached one another, Jacob braced for a fight. When they finally got close enough to speak to one another, Esau hugged Jacob in a tight embrace and they both wept. Jacob introduced Esau to his wives and daughters, who all bowed when they met Esau. In Chapter 36, Esau and Jacob bury their father together. This is grace, in all its tenderness. It is just as strong as it is tender. In this moment, Esau showcases what it means to be strong and soft at the same time.

Just as Esau extended it to Jacob, so have you been extended grace. Jesus himself offers grace to you daily. The beautiful thing about grace is it's always available to you, even in the midst of a weak-hearted moment. Guilt and shame fool us into thinking that we can't seek God when we've made a mistake or hurt someone. It is in those moments that we need to seek God most desperately. It is in those moments that we need Christ's transformative grace the most so that we can best love ourselves, our neighbors, and God, even if it means learning that we were wrong.

That's what I believe is the strongest lesson of this text: God's grace is stronger than our weak hearts. When we do something that hurts ourselves or our neighbor, God's grace helps us seek accountability, ask for forgiveness, and grow into stronger, more Christ-like people. It doesn't matter if we've got the body of a workout fanatic, a limp noodle, or anything in between—the strength God cares about is our ability to grow into more compassionate people.

And that is a beautiful strength indeed.

Reflection Questions

- Think of a word in English that has many different uses (Ex. "I love my partner" versus "I love pizza."). How does using one word to explain two radically different concepts make communication complicated?

- How does the distinction between "feminine" and "weak-hearted" affect how you read this passage? How does it affect your willingness to embrace your own femininity, regardless of your gender identity and expression?

- Think about a recent conflict where you or the other person involved sought confirmation bias from someone who didn't understand the conflict. Did it help resolve the conflict? What could have been a more positive way to handle it?

- What is a weak-hearted moment you experienced recently? How did you find the courage to seek God's grace?

- How have you witnessed the transformative power of grace in your life or in the life of a loved one?

Prayer:

Lord of all Creation, of all people of all nations, grow in us a humble spirit. Help us be more committed to showing your love than we are to winning an argument. In the moments when we mess up, give us the courage to seek both your face and the face of those we've wronged so that we may repent. Let us never be too prideful to admit when we were wrong and, in all things, keep our hearts ever-open to your transformative grace. Amen.

Interlude: Grace in Love

Scripture reading as a spiritual practice? I have to admit I've never been very consistent in that practice. Growing up in a conservative Baptist household, I internalized scripture reading as a pathway to validation from myself, from authority figures, and even from God. The more I read and the more verses I could recite, the "better" I was. I regularly saw scripture used to condemn others first, and seldom self—except the platitudes of "grace for this sinner." The Bible was wielded as a weapon against people in the community, and I saw firsthand the harm that caused to people I cared about. I saw how it pushed them further from any opportunity to meet and truly know Jesus.

What stuck with me most was the fear—fear that if we didn't follow everything the Bible "clearly" laid out for us, then we would suffer. We would suffer in life, we would miss out on "God's best" for us. We would suffer in death, have "less" reward in heaven, or lead those around us to spend eternity in hell because of our own shortcomings interpreting scripture. I think some only know how to bring people to Jesus by scaring them first, and then offering Jesus as a solution. I don't mean to imply that Jesus isn't a refuge or full of grace—I have experienced that love, grace, and comfort throughout my life, even when I fell away from church and Bible reading. My faith in the church faltered, although my faith in Christ himself never wavered. But that fear never quite left me, and I don't know if it ever will. I suspect I will always carry some amount of terror that how I read and understand the Word of God will eternally condemn my loved ones who are not Christians because I didn't properly share the gospel with them.

That fear and conservative upbringing kept me from realizing that I might be bisexual until my late college years. Even then my own viewpoint on being gay shifted from believing it was a choice to believing that people may be born that way but it was a sinful temptation to be overcome. Then I began to cultivate a more diverse friend group with non-cishet people. I learned different understandings of scripture based on the original languages and context. I read what I could and prayerfully weighed it against what I had been taught growing up. I began to understand being gay as just another facet of the beautiful diversity of creation.

As a not-entirely-out bisexual woman in a straight-passing marriage, I will rarely experience the judgment and condemnation so often brought down on others whose true expression of love is less safe than my own. I'm blessed to have loving friends who remind me that doesn't make my experience any less valid, and I wouldn't hesitate to offer that same encouragement to someone else walking a similar path. I hope that one day I'll be able to read scripture without the shadow of that fear and accompanying guilt, and I hope others who have similar experiences will also share that freedom. If not today, then maybe one day.

Amanda West Wilkerson (she/her)
A Bisexual Christian

Note

[1] Matthew Vines, *God and the Gay Christian: The Biblical Case in Support of Same-Sex Relationships* (New York: Convergent Books, 2014), 119.

Chapter 9

Proper Law

"This means understanding that the law is laid down not for the innocent but for the lawless and disobedient… for exploiters,[1] slave traders, liars, perjurers, and whatever else is contrary to the sound teaching."—1 Timothy 1:9-10

When I was a kid, I loved the story of Robin Hood, particularly Disney's retelling of it—who doesn't love foxes? His marksmanship for archery was awe-inspiring and he seemed like the perfect adventurer. He was always taking money from the villains in order to give it to people who needed it. Every time he brought gold, food, or other goods to a family in need, they showered Robin Hood with gratitude. Even from a young age, I could tell that Robin Hood's actions allowed these families to survive another day. He was a hero in every sense of the word.

It wasn't until I was older that I realized that Robin Hood was breaking the law by stealing the gold and giving it to those families. Not only was he breaking the law, he was stealing directly from law enforcement (the sheriff of Nottingham) and the law maker (Prince John). He saw that the law was not good and broke it, regularly putting himself at risk to get that gold and give it back to the impoverished citizens of Nottingham. As an adult, I can now appreciate the subversive nature of Robin Hood's vigilante justice.

Now that I'm older, one character strikes my interest more than he ever has: Prince John.

Prince John was only temporarily in charge, overseeing things while his brother King Richard the Lionheart fought in the Crusades. If King Richard was a good king, Prince John was the most opposite you could get. Spoiled, selfish, and apathetic to the needs of his people, Prince John levied criminally high taxes on the common folk of Nottingham in order to satiate his greed. His greed for what? Everything: gold, gems, fine foods, fancy clothes, and other vices of the flesh, all at the expense of his—actually, his brother's—citizens. He cared little—if at all—if his citizens were well-fed and housed. He only paid the citizens any mind if they couldn't pay the new taxes. If they couldn't pay the fines, he ordered them to be imprisoned and set astronomically high bail for their release.

As awful as all of these things were, John did them in such a way that they were technically legal. There were no laws indicating a cap on how high he could drive taxes, no laws saying he couldn't take food or shelter from families unable to pay the taxes. He twisted the law to make it a tool for his selfish desires. Legally, no one could touch him because, legally, he did "nothing" wrong.

As I've preached before and will preach again, legality does not dictate morality.

I think that the example set forth in Robin Hood reflects reality, particularly in America today. Across the country, things like predatory lending are crippling Americans' ability to remain debt-free. Bail costs are set unreasonably high for people who commit petty crimes—not to mention the disparity between the bails of White folks and Black folks who commit the same crime. Across the country, Black folks' bail is set higher than their White counterparts who committed the same or similar crimes. In this case, the law is not always used properly and, as a result, many people suffer for a few people's gain.

But what does this commentary—or a story about a furry orange vigilante—have to do with the story that 1 Timothy tells? More than one might think. A lot more.

In 1 Timothy, Paul is writing to Timothy concerning the misuse of doctrine in the city of Ephesus. In the beginning of the letter, Paul urges Timothy to find the ones teaching false things in order to stop them from teaching "meaningless talk" and things they know nothing about.

Essentially, he's trying to make sure that the community isn't overrun with lies about the personhood and character of Jesus.

I wonder what those false teachers' intentions were. Scholars aren't sure who they were or why they were teaching,[2] but I can bet we can make some guesses to their motivations. I imagine that most of those people honestly had good intentions. Maybe they heard the hope in the Gospel message and were overcome with desire to share the Good News, even if they did not understand it.

> **A Word About Missions**
>
> As someone who studied ministry at the undergraduate and graduate levels with the intention of becoming a missionary, missions has a special place in my heart. I think mission trips and acts of charity can be done well if they are done in collaboration with the people you aim to serve—as opposed to you forcing your projects and doctrines on them. I've included some resources at the end of this book if you're curious to explore that idea further.

If that was the case, they probably didn't realize their words were causing more harm than good.

Those kinds of well-meaning, false teachers are still around today, often in the form of American evangelical missionaries. Overcome with the desire to serve "the least of these," these missionaries will often go to some of the most remote regions of the world and try to change civilizations without realizing the harm they cause to the communities. I vividly remember a story one of my undergraduate professors told us in class about one such mission trip that he had been a part of, and one such missionary so desperate to do good. She was so desperate to "save" the children of the village that she volunteered to teach the Sunday school lesson for that trip. So, she stood up in front of a group of children between the ages of 5-8 and said something along the lines of, "Right now, if you died, you would all go to Hell because you don't believe in Jesus. Jesus can save you from Hell, but only if you accept Jesus in your heart as your Lord and Savior. Who here wants Jesus to be your Savior?" All of the children raised their hands.

Thank goodness there's more to the story.

The kids in the village only spoke Spanish and this missionary only spoke English, so my professor acted as the translator ... kind of. Here was his "translation": "Jesus loves you very much. He would love to be your forever-friend. Who here wants to be forever-friends with Jesus?" Thank goodness for quick-thinking professors.

That missionary obviously did not mean the kids harm, but her misunderstanding about the teachings of Christ's love could have done serious emotional and psychological harm to those kids, as evidenced by young and middle aged adults today citing childhood stories like that as major contributing factors to their religious trauma. That damage is a consequence of a well-meaning person teaching on something they know nothing about, but confidently affirm.

While I imagine that the well-meaning, unintentional harm-doer is one kind of person that Paul is talking about in 1 Timothy, I imagine that there is also another group of people spouting false teachings about the Gospel. This group, though, may have included people who intentionally twisted the words of the Gospel for their own selfish gain. Maybe they did so because they wanted to elevate their social status. Maybe they only taught part of the scripture in order to oppress others—like not teaching the story of Exodus to their slaves, which happened in plantations across the South before the Civil War. Maybe they used the Gospel to line their own pockets at the expense of the widow and the orphan. As much as I believe most of these false teachers Paul mentions had good but misguided intentions, I believe that there were some who used the Gospel as a means to gain power, not share love.

We don't have to Google news stories too long before we find present-day examples of people who use the law for their own selfish desires at the expense of others, both inside the Church and in society as a whole. Some use the law to deny rights to countless groups of people simply because they aren't White, straight, or male. Some use the law to hoard more wealth than they'll ever need in this life while their neighbors go hungry or get crushed by predatory lending. Some use the law to invalidate provable facts. I could go on and on. Regardless of the century, there are people who have used and will continue to use both the law and the Gospel for their own selfish gain.

Paul has little patience for false teachers, no matter their intentions. In this letter, he reminds Timothy that the whole point of the law is to keep the law-breakers—like those who twist the law for their own gain—in line. He then lists the kinds of people the law is supposed to keep in line: lawless and disobedient, the godless and the sinful, the unholy and the murderers of their parents, the fornicators, the exploiters, the slave traders, the liars, and the perjurers. Based on the breadth of this list, I'd be willing to bet that Paul puts the false teachers on the list somewhere between the liars and the murderers.

So what's the lesson for us in this passage? I think most of us are onboard with not twisting the law for our own selfish gain, and that's a good lesson to take from this text. But I also believe there's another, powerful lesson hidden in this text. If we go back to verse 3, we see that Paul starts his message to Timothy with a plea: "I urge you, as I did when I was on my way to Macedonia, to remain in Ephesus so that you may instruct certain people not to teach any different doctrine, and not to occupy themselves with myths and endless genealogies rather than the divine training that is known by the faith."

Paul is begging Timothy to protect both the law and the Gospel, and the truth of Christ's love therein. He's asking Timothy to stand between the lies and God's people, much like my professor stood between the words of that missionary and those children that fateful day—or even as Robin Hood stood between Prince John and the people of Nottingham. Paul is calling Timothy to help protect others from the hurt that happens when we misrepresent the Gospel, and I believe God calls us to the same work.

What truths are we called to protect? Jesus taught so many things. It can be intimidating to be a protector of truth when we're not entirely sure of it ourselves. What keeps us from being like the first group of people, the people who mean well but unintentionally do harm? Where do we start?

I'd say we should start with whatever Jesus said was most important.

At my church The Faith Community, our guiding principle is the Greatest Commandment. Our Lead Pastor Kristian (mentioned in the previous chapter) even went so far as to curate an entire theological framework around it called Greatest Commandment Theology. What that means for us and our ministry is that if an action or teaching shows love to ourselves and our neighbors, then it will show love to God and we should do or teach that thing. If it doesn't show love to ourselves or our neighbors, then it won't show love to God and we shouldn't do or teach that thing. It's a simple framework to understand, but a challenging one to live day-to-day. That said, we believe that it is worth hanging our entire faith on because Jesus himself said that "on these two command-ments hang all the laws and prophets" (Matthew 22:40). If we focus on those three things—loving God, our neighbors, and ourselves—and protect those things, then all the other things will fall into place.

When we see others using the Gospel to hurt others—intentionally or unintentionally—we know that it's not an act of love. If we take Paul's charge to Timothy as our own, then we know that we are also called to stand between the harm and those hurting in order to realize Christ's love in this broken world. It's hard work, and sometimes it's painful work. But it is the work that we have to do if we ever hope to see Christ's prayer of the Kindom of God "on earth as it is in heaven" realized in our lifetime.

So, grab your gear and tell Robin Hood to wait up. It's time to get the Good News back to the people from whom it was stolen. Let's get to work.

Reflection Questions

- Can you remember a time when you tried to help, but ended up hurting the people you were trying to help? What was that experience like for you? For them?

- Think of a time you've seen someone twist the truth for their own gain. How did it hurt everyone involved? What was the reconciliation process like, if there was one?

- What does it mean for you to stand between the lies and God's people?

- How does the Greatest Commandment influence your daily life?

Prayer:

Lord of all Creation, of every person of every nation, grow in us a courageous spirit. Let us be willing to dig deep for truths that aren't always on the surface, but just as powerful all the same. Let us not be at peace if we are in the presence of the misuse of your love, but instead grow in us a spirit courageous enough to stand between the lies and the hurting. Amen.

Interlude: Risen Indeed

You'd think, as a gay man, I'd love Easter. It's flamboyant, it's colorful, the outfits are on point, flowers are everywhere, and it's all to celebrate a man's coming out experience that is more readily embraced and accepted by the women in his life than the men. So, any given Tuesday for LGBTQ+ people.

But not this year. Easter 2015 saw me praising Good Friday and having a hell of a time—pun intended—joining in the hallelujah chorus and repeating, with any joy, "He is risen, indeed!"

In fact, that particular Easter, I'd rather Jesus have stayed dead.

My reasoning then was that Jesus' resurrection, however indirectly, led to the spiritual and church trauma I was experiencing. I had come out just two years prior and was still sifting through chummy, scuzzy waters of identity crisis.

I knew for sure most Christians didn't want me, so why would I want to be a Christian?

I knew for sure that, however many Bible verses there were that spoke broadly of justice and concern for the minoritized, there were precisely zero that spoke specifically about justice for me and my queer siblings.

If you're looking for an explicitly pro-queer Bible verse, you will not find it.

But if you're looking for, in most post-RSV translations, an explicitly anti-queer Bible verse, well, heck, you'll find at least six. Or seven. Or maybe even eight, depending on how hetero you're feeling that day.

Which brings me back to the balcony at First Baptist Church, Jefferson City, Tennessee, on Easter Sunday 2015. Jesus did not once say, "Come to me, those who are eunuchs and those who love people who are similarly endowed"—or whatever other Bible-y phrase could correlate.

To me, Jesus was the root cause of this religion that was now killing me mentally and killing my friends—physically—all over the globe.

Jesus did precious little to mitigate the harm that would later be caused by the religion bearing his name. And I wanted him to apologize for it. I wanted him to emerge from the tomb and into accountability, to stare in the face the reality that queer people don't have the luxury of rising on the third day.

Jesus got a second chance. We don't.

Had I known in 2015 that the clobber verses could not simply be explained with M.Div.-level theologizing, but, indeed, could be redeemed, I might have been more prone to celebrate Jesus's return to this mortal coil.

Had I known in 2015 that Jesus likely wouldn't repeat the clobber verses, either—he was pretty choosy with this Hebrew Scriptures, after all—I probably would have seen him more as an ally than an antagonist.

I didn't know that, though. And so, Easter Sunday 2015 stands as the Easter I wished Jesus didn't get back up.

I hope and pray I, or anyone else, never gets to that point again.

Grayson Hester (he/him)
A Gay and Queer Christian

Notes

[1] It is important to highlight two highly contentious words that Paul uses in this passage: *pornea* and *arsenokoitai*. Many conservative scholars translate *arsenokoitai* as "homosexuals," though this word does not show up in any other writings of the time; that means we have no writings outside a handful of Paul's letters to compare this word to in order to confirm the validity of its translation as "homosexuals." Many moderate and progressive scholars point to this word's relationship to the word *malakoi* or "the sexual exploitation of young boys by adult men" to suggest that "sexual exploiters" might be a more accurate translation. This argument is made that much stronger when we consider that this word is surrounded by words that translate to things like "slave traders," "liars," and "perjurers" in 1 Timothy. For that reason, I replaced "sodomite" with "exploiters" in this chapter. As far as *pornea* is concerned, the vast majority of scholars agree that it and its relative *pornoi* are blanket terms for "sexual immorality," not a reference to any specific sexual activity. For more on these word studies, check out the resources at the end of this book.

James V. Brownson, *Bible, Gender, Sexuality: Reframing the Church's Debate on Same-Sex Relationships* (Grand Rapids, MI/Cambridge, UK: William B. Eerdmans Publishing Company, 2013), 42-43.

[2] Robert W. Wall with Richard B. Steele, *1 & 2 Timothy and Titus*, The Two Horizons New Testament Commentary, ed. Joel B. Green and Max Turner (Grand Rapids, MI/Cambridge, UK: William B. Eerdmans Publishing Company, 2012), 63.

Chapter 10

Something's Missing

"Likewise, Sodom and Gomorrah and the surrounding cities, which, in the same manner as they, indulged in sexual immorality and pursued unnatural lust, serve as an example by undergoing a punishment of eternal fire."—Jude 7

When I was growing up, I heard many lectures from my parents on keeping family struggles "in the family." If I needed to talk to someone about any kind of family conflict, I was not allowed to talk with a friend or trusted adult outside of the family; moreover, I would be reprimanded for doing so, and was on several occasions. That paradigm for dealing with struggles led to a toxic, codependent family structure. Obviously, this wasn't a healthy environment to curate a good framework for conflict resolution.

When I got to college, I had the opportunity to move beyond that toxic system. I met amazing people and cultivated friendships with people who poured into my life in powerful, meaningful ways. As we got closer, I shared with them the struggles my family faced, and that I had faced within that family system. They validated for me a lot of the toxicity and challenges I experienced growing up. It was liberating to know that I wasn't a bad person for wanting to be treated well. Through them and their families, I also got to see snapshots of healthier family systems, systems that knew how to better manage conflict

> **A Word About Chosen Family**
>
> In the LGBTQIA+ community, we've often felt the sting of blood relatives excluding us from the family. As a result, we've created the idea of chosen family out of necessity. More often than not, the people we rely on, celebrate with, and on whose shoulders we cry have no blood relation to us but are our dearest family. It's one of the most beautiful things about the LGBTQIA+ community. We are able to adapt to make the support networks we need in order to cultivate wholeness. Who constitutes family in your life?

My biological family was not pleased at the fact that I was "airing the family's dirty laundry" to my friends. They were also not pleased that I sometimes chose to spend holiday breaks with my friends instead of my biological family in order to avoid that toxicity. In their attempts to guilt me to come home, they'd say several things. They'd say, "Friends come and go, but family lasts forever," or, most often, "Blood runs thicker than water." The people who share your genes should be closer to you than anyone else in your life, especially if you've only known those outside of the family for a short time.

I sat with that phrase "blood runs thicker than water" for a long time; it just wasn't true for me. I remember feeling like I was "on the outside looking in" a lot growing up, especially in middle school and high school. Don't get me wrong, I loved my biological family and still do. I just never felt like I was on the same wavelength as them. Was something wrong with me?

In recent years, though, I learned that the phrase "blood is thicker than water" is actually better translated as "the blood of the covenant runs thicker than the water of the womb."[1] The relationships you choose are stronger than the ones you are born with.[2] The origin of that phrase is complicated. Some scholars trace it back to ancient Gaelic roots in a 1180 epic poem called "Reynard the Fox." The proverb alludes to the fact that those you shed blood with in battle are closer to you than those you grew up with in your family.[3] Other scholars point to an ancient Middle East saying of a similar bent (blood runs thicker than milk) to highlight that the people you fight alongside in battle are closer to you than your biological family.[4] Regardless of the origin, the sentiment is the same: Sometimes, the family you choose is closer to you than the family you're born into.

By omitting some words, the phrase took on a completely different meaning. In fact, the actual phrase means the exact opposite of how most people use it today.

Upon this discovery, I was shocked—but also relieved. The actual phrase validated my lived experience, and it was liberating to let go of the shame associated with the lie I'd been told. Not only did it validate my lived experience, but it helped me feel less alone. Other people felt the same way I did, and they felt strongly enough about it to record it in writing.

I think it's important to note that the people in my life who have misquoted this phrase haven't done so intentionally. They honestly think that the phrase is simply "blood runs thicker than water" and that it means biological family relationships are most important. The fact that it validates their lived experience makes it feel like a truth or fact to them. If it rings true for you, why question it? What's the point? This reality made me wonder how many people have been hurt by the misuse of this phrase. More pressing than that, it also made me wonder how many people had been hurt because they internalized that misinterpretation like I had.

Why bring up the systemic misquotation and misuse of this phrase? Because sometimes the lesson isn't in the phrase itself, but it's in how the phrase is used. In this case, the lesson is that by removing a few key pieces of this phrase, the meaning of it changes completely.

We see the exact same thing happen in the Bible. Sometimes, later authors of the Bible misquote earlier authors of the Bible in order to argue their point. Whether those misquotations were intentional or accidental, we may never know. Does that make scripture unholy or unreliable? Honestly, I don't think so. Those passages still contain valuable truths for us to learn, just not in the way we thought. Instead of taking the text at face value, it requires us to examine it more closely and to see how that misquote affected the surrounding community. It takes more work to examine the context like this, but the reward we reap is that much richer as a result. As my friend Kristian says, "If you take a text out of its context, all you're left with is a con."

With that in mind, let's dig into what the book of Jude has to teach us. The lessons here may be just as much in what wasn't said as they might be in what was.

The book of Jude was written around the same time as 2 Peter (just before 150 C.E.) and the purpose of the book was noble. The author was writing to these Jesus followers because a heretical group in the community had started telling people in the church that Jesus was only divine and, therefore, could not be human.[5] To our modern eye, that may not seem a big concern. Some people started a rumor—so what? What's the big deal?

Well—a lot. Jesus being simultaneously human and divine is what made him different from the deities of other religions of the time, particularly the pagan religions of Rome. If you studied Ancient Rome in your Ancient Civilizations or World History class, then you know that Roman mythology was extremely complicated, and not just because of who was the god or goddess of what thing and so forth. The interpersonal relationships between the gods among themselves and between various humans were messy. I mean "my god hates your god so our cities are at war with each other" messy. I mean "Jupiter disguised himself as a swan to cheat on his wife with a mortal woman" messy. I mean "humanity will suffer because the deities can't figure out how to get along" messy. Seriously, if you're into soap operas, Roman or Greek mythology would be right up your alley.

By removing Jesus of his humanity, that separates him from us and puts him on a similar level as the Roman deities: a divine being so disconnected from humanity that he doesn't care if humanity suffers. That idea is so antithetical to who Jesus is because Jesus suffered with and for us. Taking away that key component of Christ's identity changes the message of the Gospel into something unrecognizable. If we separate Jesus from his own humanity, we sever the connection between Jesus and humanity as a whole.

So as the author of Jude moves past the introduction of his letter, he's reminding the people what happened to ancestors who misused or misrepresented God's word in the world. "Now I desire to remind you, though you are fully informed, that the Lord, who once for all saved a people out of the land of Egypt, afterward destroyed those who did not believe. And the angels who did not keep their own position, but left their proper dwelling, he has kept in eternal chains in deepest darkness for the judgment of the great day. Likewise, Sodom and Gomorrah and the surrounding cities, which, in the same manner as they, indulged in sexual immorality and pursued unnatural lust, serve as an example by undergoing a punishment of eternal fire."

Essentially, the author of Jude reminds the members of the community that there are dire consequences for misrepresenting God through false teachings. In his haste to provide instruction and encouragement to this community, he left out quite a few details about the Exodus, as well as the destruction of Sodom and Gomorrah.

If we remember the context surrounding Sodom and Gomorrah as discussed in Chapter 2, we know that the sin of Sodom and Gomorrah was their radical hostility, their disregard for those in need, and their desire to rape the angels disguised as men. Moreover, Isaiah, Jeremiah, and Ezekiel confirm that Sodom and Gomorrah's sins were pride, arrogance, disregard for the poor, and an utter lack of hospitality. Not to read Jesus into the Hebrew Bible, but the prophets are essentially saying that the people of Sodom and Gomorrah were against everything Jesus represents.

For Jude's brevity, I think it's also important to remember his audience. His readers were most likely Jewish followers of Jesus who were familiar with important Hebrew stories, as evidenced by the fact that he also referenced ancient Jewish stories and sources that aren't in the Christian Bible as we have it today.[6] He wouldn't need to go into detail about the events of the Exodus or Sodom and Gomorrah because his audience would already know the stories and know them well. It would be like if I said, "better not pout, better not cry" to some children, they don't need me to say anything else to know I'm referencing the fact that Santa will know if they've been good this year.

Over time and after countless translations, it seems that a game of Telephone has occurred with this text. In our context, we are missing something that would be plain as day to the readers of the time. Just like with the phrase "the blood of covenant is thicker than the water of the womb," we've missed the point because we are missing key words. When we understand the context, it becomes clear that the letter of Jude is a beautiful, powerful call to action to defend Christ's humanity.

What does it mean that Christ was human and not just divine? Through Jesus, God became human. Like the scripture says in the Gospel of John, "In the beginning was the Word, and the Word was with God, and the Word was God … and the Word became flesh and lived among us." God experienced all of the ups and downs, joys and sorrows, hurt and healing that come with being human. Through the life of Jesus, God gets to connect with humanity on a carnal level that is otherwise unthinkable. Because Jesus was human, we serve a God who knows what it's like to deal with grief. We serve a God who knows what it's like to fear for his own life. We serve a God who knows what it is to be hungry, tired, and thirsty—and what it feels like to have those needs met. We serve a God who knows what it's like to have to rely on the kindness of strangers for his next meal. We serve a God who knows how to deal with anger, sadness, elation, and frustration, often all in the same day.

Because Jesus was human as well as divine, we serve a God who knows how it feels to live this mundane, sacred thing we call life. We can take comfort in the fact that when we come to Jesus with a problem, we know—without a shadow of a doubt—that he gets it. And that truth is worth protecting.

Reflection Questions:

- Recall a time when you only told part of a story to a friend, intentionally or unintentionally. How did it affect everyone involved?

- Think about a time that someone shared a rumor or half-truth about you. How did it affect your relationship with that person and everyone who heard the rumor? By the time it got back to you, how had the story changed?

- How does Christ's humanity affect your ability to connect with the Divine? Does it make that connection easier?

- How do you see your own humanity reflected in Christ's humanity?

Prayer

Lord of all Creation, of every person of every nation, grow in us a curious spirit. Let us always be willing to look for deeper truths as we seek your wisdom. In our searching, help us not be satisfied with partial truths because they confirm our biases. Instead, challenge us to seek instruction beyond the surface level. Help us consider all of your words even while we examine just a few. Let us be ever-thirsty for your wisdom, especially if it isn't explicitly written in the scriptures we read. Amen.

Interlude: The Bigger Picture

I grew up Pentecostal, and scripture was used as both a tool of spiritual inspiration and a weapon of identity destruction. I was taught that anything that had to do with understanding life and how to live a "righteous" one was to be found in scripture. For many years, I both loved and feared scripture reading. As I perused the delicately lined pages, I would fall deeper and deeper in a hole of self-loathing and flagellation. I paid penance because of scripture reading and, moreover, after being "enlightened" by spiritual leaders. My relationship with the Bible was shaky. The Bible was that guy on that app that you found physically appealing, was totally not healthy for you, but you stuck around anyway because, well, you didn't know anything better was out there.

After years of struggling and, eventually, reconciling my faith and sexual orientation, I revisited Bible reading with extreme hesitation. I wanted to connect more with my faith, but I was afraid I would return back to those days of self-condemnation. After I started attending seminary, I had so many "a-ha!" moments. It was then that I started to read the texts not as a tool of instruction for how to live a "righteous" life, but as a literary source to illustrate the complex ideologies and social locations represented in the text. I started to understand the fallacies found and some universal truths in the message of Jesus. As a queer person, I was reading text with a critical eye—something that was frowned upon by my church of origin. I delved deeper into my studies by reading outside Biblical sources who wrote on liberation and queer theology. I found healing in my reading!

I find importance in reading scripture through the lens of a queer Person of Color because I find freedom in critiquing it. It is through this deliberative theology that I can reclaim scripture reading as a spiritual practice. I read it through the eyes of a queer, Gender Non-Conforming, Latinx multi- and inter-faith minister. I read it through the lens of a wounded child seeking comfort. I read it to find my truth—and whatever does not resonate with me, just does not. I can now choose to accept what works and leave the rest, without feeling like I am going to live in eternal damnation. I once wrote that one of my favorite ways of disrupting and resisting queerphobia is worshipping in rejecting spaces. Reclaiming scripture reading it in a new way that works for me allows me to disrupt the "norm" and offer a space for safe internal and external dialogue. It has been the impetus to my spiritual maturation.

Robert D. Arnáu ("he"/they)
A Queer and Gender Non-Conforming Christian

Notes

[1] The origin of this phrase is complicated, and it seems that many cultures have an ancient proverb that communicates a similar idea. See the understanding of covenant in the times of Old Testament and other Ancient Near East societies.

[2] "Blood is thicker than water," in *The Oxford Dictionary of Proverbs*, ed. by J. A. Simpson and Jennifer Speake (Oxford: Oxford University Press, 2015), 31.

[3] See Johann Wolfgang von Goethe, *Reynard the Fox*, trans. Hjalmar Hjorth Boyesen (Scotts Valley, CA: CreateSpace Independent Publishing Platform, 2015).

[4] See H. Clay Trumbull, *The Blood Covenant: A Primitive Rite and Its Bearing on Scripture* (Charleston, SC: Nabu Press, 2010), 5.

[5] Albert E. Barnett, "Jude: Introduction," in *The Interpreter's Bible: A Commentary in Twelve Volumes*, vol. VII, ed. George Arthur Buttrick (Nashville: Abingdon Press, 1957), 319.

[6] Albert E. Barnett and Elmer G. Homrighausen, "Jude: Text, Exegesis, and Exposition," in *The Interpreter's Bible: A Commentary in Twelve Volumes*, vol. VII, ed. George Arthur Buttrick (Nashville: Abingdon Press, 1957), 327.

Conclusion

Our Place at the Table

"And the eunuch said, 'Look, here is water! What is to prevent me from being baptized?'... the eunuch saw him no more, and went on his way rejoicing."
—Acts 8:36, 39

One of my favorite authors is Pastor Nadia Bolz-Weber. She's rugged, smart-mouthy, and unafraid to use a few choice words to drive the point of a message home. The things that she has accomplished in the church she founded and the books she's penned have blazed a trail for people like me to be able to do the kinds of ministry I do. I listen to her sermons regularly and have all of her books on my shelves. If I were forced to pick a favorite, it's a two-way tie between *Accidental Saints* and *Shameless*—but please don't make me choose. I love them because they make my mind and my spirit think deeply about the Divine.

Her earlier book *Pastrix* is right up there on my list of favorite books of all time. In a book that's part practical theology and part memoir, Nadia tells the story of how she became called to be a pastor, recounts her experience of being a recovering addict, and shares some of her highest highs and lowest lows in ministry. I first read it during one of my early years in seminary. As a then-closeted woman with a calling to ministry, I related to so many of the struggles she described. This book encouraged me to keep fighting the good fight, to keep pursuing my calling no matter who would be upset by my queerness.

In this book, she includes a story about preparing a sermon on the story of Philip and the Ethiopian eunuch. She suggests that, while the story of the Ethiopian eunuch is a powerful story about who all is included in the Kindom of God—and, in her estimation, perfect sermon material for every progressive pastor who wants to preach on diversity and inclusion—perhaps the bigger lesson is in fact Philip's conversion. Philip had to change something within himself in order to baptize someone "different" into the church, a someone he would probably have never baptized otherwise. In Nadia's commentary of this text, she proposes that the Holy Spirit had to work in Philip so that he could be a better neighbor, a better follower of Jesus.[1]

The first time I read Nadia's take on that story, I loved it. As a then-closeted, baby progressive Christian, that interpretation gave me hope. I hadn't yet come out to many people. There were a few people I was particularly worried about telling: people who had housed me for a season, who all but adopted me when I was in college. Nadia's take on the passage gave me hope that, like with Philip, the Holy Spirit could move in their lives in such a way that they, too, would realize that I belong in the Kindom of God just as I am. Perhaps it was a naive hope, but it's a hope I clung to nonetheless.

That first reading of *Pastrix* was probably in 2014 or 2015. When I reread *Pastrix* during the long quarantine caused by the COVID-19 pandemic, I was eager to discover how these insights resonated with me now that I had a few years of ministry experience under my belt.

When I came across this chapter with different eyes, though, something felt ... off. Sure, reading Acts 8:26-40 as the conversion of a religious leader who opens himself up to the possibility that he'd been wrong is a good reading of this text, but is it the strongest? Is that really the best lesson we can take from this text? Let's examine the story ourselves.

In the story, the Ethiopian eunuch (let's call them[2] "Sam") was returning from Jerusalem, where they had traveled to worship. That one line in the passage is crucial to this narrative. If we remember the commentary around Deuteronomy 23:1 from Chapter 5, we know that Sam would not have been allowed inside the temple grounds to worship—they would have been forced to stay in the outer gardens. They wouldn't have been allowed into the places closer to the altar, but they loved God enough—knew God loved them enough—to travel from Ethiopia to Jerusalem to worship at the temple anyway. How many of us have shown up to church to worship God, even though we knew the assembly wouldn't embrace us, would relegate us to the outer edges of the activities? I resonate with Sam here.

So Sam is returning home from what was probably a hard, emotionally challenging trip to Jerusalem when they stop to read part of a passage from the book of Isaiah: "Like a sheep he was led to the slaughter, and like a lamb silent before its shearer, so he does not open his mouth. In his humiliation justice was denied him. Who can describe his generation? For his life is taken away from the earth." Sam was puzzled by the verses and, because Philip just happened to be walking by, asked Philip to explain those verses to them. Philip explains that those verses foretell the coming, crucifixion, and resurrection of Jesus and shares the Good News with Sam. They traveled together for a while—the scripture passage does not specify how long—and came across some water. When Sam sees the water, they ask, "What is to prevent me from being baptized?" Sam and

Philip stop the chariot, get out, and Philip baptizes Sam. The Holy Spirit then snatches Philip away, and Sam goes on their way rejoicing.

Other than the Holy Spirit literally snatching Philip away, one thing has always puzzled me about this story: What happened between the time Philip explained the verses to Sam and the moment they came across the water? How long did they travel together? The passage simply doesn't tell us. Did Philip spend the whole time explaining those two verses to Sam? If they were traveling together for hours, that'd be a long time to discuss two verses. Maybe Sam asked Philip question after question, trying to understand exactly who this Jesus person really was.

Or perhaps Sam and Philip were a bit more introverted. Maybe once Philip explained those two verses, Sam returned their focus to reading the scriptures because Sam wanted to learn more. Back then, the passages of scripture weren't in books, but on long scrolls that you constantly have to unroll at the right and reroll at the left in order to keep it at a manageable length to hold. So Sam would need to unroll a little more from the right in order to continue his study of this sacred text.

Here's the kicker: The verses that Sam was reading come from Isaiah 53:7-8. You know what's pretty darn close to Isaiah 53, especially since they were likely on the same long scroll? Isaiah 56:3-5: "Do not let the foreigner joined to the LORD say, 'The LORD will surely separate me from his people'; and do not let the eunuch say, 'I am just a dry tree.' For thus says the LORD: To the eunuchs who keep my sabbaths, who choose the things that please me and hold fast my covenant, I will give, in my house and within my walls, a monument and a name better than sons and daughters; I will give them an everlasting name that shall not be cut off."

After hearing the Good News of Jesus Christ as they were returning from Jerusalem to worship God in a place that did not welcome them, maybe Sam was utterly stunned by those three verses. Maybe they realized that Philip coming at just that time with this particular message from God, at the moment they read those verses, wasn't a coincidence. Maybe it was the confirmation Sam needed in order to know that God loved and welcomed them just as they are. Sam looks up from that message—that divine promise that God will bless them—sees water, and breaks the silence: "Philip, what's to stop me from getting baptized?" Philip freezes. Maybe Philip's mind immediately jumps to Genesis 1, concerned that Sam doesn't fit neatly into the binary of male/female but then he remembers the marshes. Maybe his mind jumps to Psalm 139, concerned that Sam's body is "broken"—but then he remembers that the passage is about the mysteries of our innermost parts, not our biology, and that he couldn't possibly know the holy mysteries hidden within Sam. Philip's eyes trail down to the scroll and see where Sam had left off. He reads Isaiah 56:3-5 for himself, looks Sam in the eye, and says, "Nothing. Come on. Let's baptize you into God's family."

In that case, the story of Acts 8:26-40 isn't about a religious leader doing the right thing—as important as that lesson is. It's about someone who has been outcast their whole life realizing the glorious, terrifying, liberating truth that God loves and accepts them just as they are. God blesses them just as they are. They don't have to change who they are in order to take their seat at God's table—God laid their place setting Godself, rainbow placemat and all. That is why Sam "went on their way rejoicing."

As important as I think Nadia's point is, our lives—LGBTQIA+ lives—don't exist solely for the spiritual transformation of straight cisgender people, in the same way that female and nonbinary lives don't exists for the spiritual transformation of cishet male people, and in the same way BIPOC lives don't exist for the spiritual transformation of White people. Those transformations are simply a byproduct of our existence, not the reason for it. LGBTQIA+ lives exist because God created them and called them good—very good. As children of the divine God, we deserve to be cherished just as we are—no more than anyone else, but certainly no less. The scriptures that we hold so dear confirm this to be true.

And so I think the biggest lesson is this: we belong. We belong in the Kindom. We belong in the sanctuary. We belong by the altar. We belong in the pulpit. We belong at the table. We belong anywhere a child of God does because that is exactly who we are.

God says that there is a place for us, for we are glorious God says we deserve to be treated hospitably, and must give hospitality in return. God says we deserve to be treated with dignity, and we must treat others the same. God says we must not listen to the deception others force onto us, and must embrace authenticity instead.

God says redemption lies in the arc of the whole picture, not just the snapshot of one moment. God says that God put holy mysteries within each of us, and those mysteries are fearfully and wonderfully made.

God says we have authority in our own lives and we must use it responsibly. God says we are given grace when we repent from weak-hearted moments.

God says we are to stand between the lies of hate and God's people, who deserve the truth of love. God says we must tell the whole story, not just part of it.

And that's what we've done here. We've told the whole story.

As we sit with the truths that were hidden in these texts, it is my fervent hope that you've found healing here. I pray that you've found growth here, that you find yourself closer to the Divine than you have been in a long time. More importantly, though, I pray that this is just the beginning for you. I pray that you will hold these blessings close and use them as momentum, giving you the courage to continually take your God-given place at the table. You are loved, child of God. And with you, God is well pleased.

Keep growing.

Notes

[1] Nadia Boltz-Weber, *Pastrix: The Cranky, Beautiful Faith of a Sinner and Saint* (New York: Jericho Books, 2013), 87-95.

[2] The passage uses "he/him" pronouns for the eunuch, but we don't know if those were the pronouns this person identified with. Out of respect to their memory, I'm using "they/them" pronouns.

Epilogue

A Benediction Meal

"And now faith, hope, and love abide, these three; and the greatest of these is love."—1 Corinthians 13:13

Leaving the Stove

You've done it. You've faced your fear of the hot stove. Cooking with this particular stove wasn't easy and there were many, many moments along the way when you seriously considered stopping mid-cook to grab your phone and order takeout, but, with the help of the Holy Spirit, you stayed. The smells wafting in from the kitchen are surprisingly inviting. It's hard to believe that foods that once made you sick to your stomach now make your mouth water in anticipation.

Now, having already set the table for your loved ones and yourself, you take a deep breath and prepare to share a feast together. It's been a while since you sat at a table like this. Do you really belong here? As you look into the eyes of your guests, you realize that they're wondering the same thing. You take a deep breath and remind yourself of the truth. You've always belonged here—it wasn't anyone else's say whether you got to stay here or be sent out.

Stomach rumbling, you pick up your fork. Your guests, just as nervous as you, do the same. It's time to start.

The Appetizer: Faith

When you placed that first piece of Genesis on your plate, you stepped out on faith—a new beginning. You chose to engage a passage and a story that have both been used to deeply hurt you, your loved ones and people you know, but you engaged them both with curious—maybe even hopeful—eyes. What you taste now is a story about the importance of hospitality. Maybe it reminds you of the times you'd felt the sharp sting of rejection. Maybe it reminds you of the times that your whole, authentic self was welcomed in a warm embrace. As you take a bite, you feel the gentle warmth extend from your mouth all the way down to your toes. Its warmth reminds you of all the times you've been tightly hugged—a universal message of holistic welcome in this space. You know that there's a place for you at this table, for you are glorious.

Encouraged by what a small taste of this journey was like, you look down to see an unexpectedly clean plate, and the plates of your loved ones are clean, too. This reclamation dinner is off to a surprisingly good start! Taste buds tingling, you clear the plates and bring out the main course. You hope that the momentum will keep going throughout the remainder of the evening.

The Entrée: Hope

This course is a bit bigger than you expected, but how full of nourishment! Each component is a small, nutrient-dense adventure that requires you and your guests to chew long and swallow slowly; not like a quick drink of milk. Some bites take a while to chew, particularly that side of Leviticus. That specific dish has been shoved unceremoniously down your throat more times than you could count. Like boiled Brussels sprouts, even the mere thought of the smell of Leviticus made you nauseated. But, like the first properly cooked Brussels sprouts you ever had —roasted, tossed in a little bit of vinegar, and served with cranberries—this serving of Leviticus is different. Instead of tasting shame and disgust, you find the strong, sharp flavors of dignity and honor. The combination is revelatory, and you realize you can never go back to Leviticus the old way again—or Brussels sprouts, for that matter.

Encouraged by how Leviticus turned out, you turn your attention to the stewed Deuteronomy—you've never enjoyed this particular dish. It's always been a deceptive side. It looks harmless, but you'd always end up with bits and pieces stuck between your teeth in the most painful, tender spots—right where that stringy dish isn't supposed to be. But the meal's gone all right so far, so you figure you might as well give it a try. It's surprisingly fresh, like you're experiencing the actual, authentic taste of this dish for the first time. To top it all off, there's no grittiness to it—it's not getting stuck in your teeth. Satisfied, you deem this dish sufficiently redeemed.

Still hungry, you select Psalm 139 next. This dish was fun to put together, resembling miniature pot pies. Because they were so small, you had to hand-roll the dough and hand-form the body of the pie; nobody's pie looks exactly the same, unique to each person gathered around the table. Excited, you use your fork to break into the pie and dig around the contents. For such a small pie, there's so much to discover! Every bite tastes different, a new mystery to roll around your palate. Even though you used similar filling for everyone's pie, you're fairly confident that they all turned out a little different. Regardless, those gathered all deem the pie a wonderfully made hit.

Pleasantly surprised by how the meal is going, you turn to the intimidating scoop of Romans 1 on your plate. At the look of it, you think back to all the meals you had as a kid that had way too much salt and garlic to be suitable for human consumption—the same way you heard, "But what about Romans 1!?" more times than you can count in conversations about LGBTQIA+ affirmation. As you take a bite, you're pleased to discover that it's actually quite tasty. It's seasoned with authority—you chuckle to yourself as you think of the cookbook by chef Mark Murphy of the same title—but it's not overpowering your palate. You realize that's because you paired authority with servant leadership, and these two play off each other beautifully to make a delectable, balanced bite.

As you move to the next part of your plate, you're caught off guard by how energized this course has made you. Can it be possible to be this full of hope, only part-way through the entrée?

You rotate your plate so that the cut of 1 Corinthians is on the side closest to you. As you chew this bite, you feel the tension leave your shoulders. It's rich, decadent, and simply sublime. With each bite, you can feel your heart strengthening as you receive forgiveness for your own weak-hearted moments. It takes a while to chew, but the more you partake, the more you feel hope filling you to the brim.

Last on the plate is that scoop of 1 Timothy. This one always had a tough exterior that you couldn't quite tolerate. When prepared properly, though, you realize that this passage is kind of like a fava bean: you're not supposed to eat the exterior. As you nibble on the inside of this verse, you feel strength and courage rise in your spirit. It tastes like compassion, and you can't wait to share this compassion with your neighbor. It's just too good to keep to yourself.

The Dessert: Love

Even though you're more full of hope than you've been in such a long time, you can't help but think something's missing. As your loved ones look at you expectantly, you realize it's time for dessert! You place the dessert plates before your guests and sit down to a plate of your own. This recipe is an old one, but as you researched it for your big reclamation cook, you realized an ingredient had been missing: a dash of truth. As you take a bite, you realize that the dash of truth made this passage decadent and much richer than it had been before. The truth that Jesus is completely human and divine solidifies your own connectedness to the Divine, both in Christ and in the Holy Spirit that resides within you. The reality that no one can change that truth may just be the most satisfying bite of the meal.

The Nightcap: Blessing

You can't believe how well the reclamation dinner went. Did your guests actually enjoy the meal? From the amount of laughter and "mmmms" you heard throughout the evening, you can only conclude that they found it as nourishing as you did. And, what's more, not a single person got burned by that stove. It was all nourishment, all blessing this evening.

As you reflect on the night full of love and laughter, you're reminded of the sacrament of breaking bread. The fact that Jesus used bread as a teaching tool always seemed a little strange, but now it makes sense. In the breaking of bread, relationships deepen. Wounds heal. Judgement dissolves. Grace abounds. And even after all the bread is gone, bottles recycled, dishes cleaned, and counter-tops wiped down, faith, hope, and love remain. Everyone gathered had been baptized in love, and, after that holy baptism, went on their way rejoicing.

Now, I leave you with this blessing: You, child of God, have been fed. May the food of this table be a healing balm for your weary soul. May you receive the love God has for you, just as you are. As you've been fed, now feed others with this same love. May it be a blessing to them in the same way it's been a blessing to you. As you revisit this feast, may your cup run over with the blessing God has prepared for you. The table is prepared, and there's always a place with your name.

Amen.

Bibliography

"9 Species of Fish that Change Gender (with Pictures)." *Wildlife Informer.* https://wildlifeinformer.com/fish-that-change-gender/ (accessed May 15, 2021).

"Annie Jones—The Esau Woman." *The Human Marvels.* https://www.thehumanmarvels.com/annie-jones-the-esau-woman/ (accessed May 16, 2021).

Avatar: The Last Airbender. Created by Michael Dante DiMartino and Bryan Konietzko. Nickelodeon Animation Studios, 2004-2008. *Netflix,* https://www.netflix.com/title/70142405.

Baldock, Kathy. *Walking the Bridgeless Canyon: Repairing the Breach between the Church and the LGBT Community.* Reno, NV: Canyonwalker Press, 2014.

Barnett, Albert E. "Jude: Introduction." In *The Interpreter's Bible: A Commentary in Twelve Volumes,* vol. VII, edited by George Arthur Buttrick, (317-320). Nashville: Abingdon Press, 1957.

Barnett, Albert E. And Elmer G. Homrighausen. "Jude: Text, Exegesis, and Exposition." In *The Interpreter's Bible: A Commentary in Twelve Volumes,* vol. VII, edited by George Arthur Buttrick, (320-343). Nashville: Abingdon Press, 1957.

Bicks, Jenny and Bill Condon. *The Greatest Showman.* Directed by Michael Gracy. Original release 2017; 20th Century Fox.

"Blood is thicker than water." In *The Oxford Dictionary of Proverbs.* Edited by J. A. Simpson and Jennifer Speake. Oxford: Oxford University Press, 2015.

Bolz-Weber, Nadia. *Pastrix: The Cranky, Beautiful Faith of a Sinner and Saint.* New York: Jericho Books, 2013.

Brownson, James V. *Bible, Gender, Sexuality: Reframing the Church's Debate on Same-Sex Relationships.* Grand Rapids, MI/Cambridge, UK: William B. Eerdmans Publishing Company, 2013.

Brueggemann, Walter. *Genesis. Interpretation: A Commentary for Teaching and Preaching,* edited by James Luther Mays. Atlanta: John Knox Press, 1982.

Brueggemann, Walter. *Deuteronomy. Abingdon Old Testament Commentaries,* edited by Patrick D. Miller. Nashville: Abingdon Press, 2001.

Centennial College. *Our Stories: First Peoples of Canada*. Pressbooks. https://ecampusontario.pressbooks.pub/indigstudies/chapter/gender-identities/ (accessed June 25, 2021).

deClaissé-Walford, Nancy L. *Introduction to the Psalms: A Song from Ancient Israel*. St. Louis, MO: Chalice Press, 2004.

de la Torre, Miguel A. *Liberating Sexuality: Justice between the Sheets*. St. Louis, MO: Chalice Press, 2016.

Etymonline: Online Etymology Dictionary. "Reclamation (noun)." https://www.etymonline.com/word/reclamation#:~:text=reclamation%20(n.),protest%22%20(see%20reclaim) (accessed June 1, 2021).

Florio, Angelica. "The Real Activist Who Inspired *The Greatest Showman*'s Bearded Lady Is So Inspiring." *Bustle*, December 22, 2017. https://www.bustle.com/p/the-actor-who-plays-the-bearded-lady-in-the-greatest-showman-has-a-message-about-self-love-7630055 (accessed May 16, 2021).

Fretheim, Terence E. *The Pentateuch*. Interpreting Biblical Texts. Edited by Gene M. Tucker. Nashville: Abingdon Press, 1996.

Gadsby, Hannah. *Hannah Gadsby: Nanette*. Directed by Jon Olb and Madeleine Parry. *Netflix*, 2018. *Netflix*, https://www.netflix.com/title/80233611.

Gunnel, Hermann. *Genesis: Translated and Interpreted by Hermann Gunkel*. Translated by Mark E. Biddle. Macon, GA: Mercury University Press, 1997.

Hartke, Austen. "The Bible and Transgender Christians." The Reformation Project Symposium in Chicago, IL. October 28, 2017. *YouTube*, 41:44, https://www.youtube.com/watch?v=zs_Baw-5ydg (accessed May 14, 2021).

Hartke, Austen. *Transforming: The Bible and the Lives of Transgender Christians*. Louisville, KY: Westminster John Knox Press, 2018.

Hawkins, Peter S. "The Psalms in Poetry." In *The Oxford Handbook of The Psalms*. Edited by William P. Brown, 99-113. Oxford: Oxford University Press, 2014.

Junior, Vic Lang'at. "How Many Species of Fish Are There?" World Facts, *World Atlas*, January 10, 2019. https://www.worldatlas.com/articles/how-many-species-of-fish-are-there.html (accessed May 15, 2021).

La Trobe University. "Secrets of a sex-changing fish revealed." *ScienceDaily*, July 10, 2019. https://www.sciencedaily.com/releases/2019/07/190710163416.htm (accessed May 15, 2021).

Khaza, Olga. "Why Straight Men Gaze at Gay Women: The Psychology Behind the Male Sexual Desire for Lesbians." The Atlantic, March 8, 2016. https://

www.theatlantic.com/health/archive/2016/03/straight-men-and-lesbian-porn/472521/ (accessed on March 27, 2021).

Knowles, Melody D. "Feminist Interpretation of the Psalms." In *The Oxford Handbook of The Psalms*. Edited by William P. Brown, 424-36. Oxford: Oxford University Press, 2014.

Martin, Colby. *UnClobber: Rethinking Our Misuse of the Bible on Homosexuality*. Louisville, KY: Westminster John Knox Press, 2016.

Matthews, Victor H. and James C. Moyer. *The Old Testament: Text and Context*, 3rd ed. Grand Rapids, MI: Baker Academic, 2012.

Miller, Patrick D. *Deuteronomy. Interpretation: A Bible Commentary for Teaching and Preaching*. Edited by Patrick D. Miller. Louisville, KY: Westminster John Knox Press, 1990.

"Number of Insects (Species and Individuals." Smithsonian. https://www.si.edu/spotlight/buginfo/bugnos (accessed May 15, 2021).

Sanders, Cody J. *A Brief Guide to Ministry with LGBTQIA Youth*. Louisville, KY: Westminster John Knox Press, 2017.

Settle, Keala and The Greatest Showman Ensemble. "This is Me." By Benj Pasek and Justin Paul. Recorded 2017. Track 7 on *The Greatest Showman: Original Motion Picture Soundtrack*. Atlantic, digital album.

Smith, Zeke. "'Survivor' Contestant Opens Up About Being Outed as Transgender (Guest Column." *The Hollywood Reporter*, April 12, 2017. https://www.hollywoodreporter.com/tv/tv-news/survivor-zeke-smith-outed-as-transgender-guest-column-991514/ (accessed June 29, 2021).

Strawn, Brent A. "Poetic Attachment: Psychology, Psycholinguistics, and the Psalms." In *The Oxford Handbook of The Psalms*. Edited by William P. Brown, 405-23. Oxford: Oxford University Press, 2014.

Survivor. Season 34, episode 6, "What Happened on Exile, Stays on Exile." Aired April 12, 2017, CBS.

Trumbull, H. Clay. *The Blood Covenant: A Primitive Rite and Its Bearing on Scripture*. Charleston, SC: Nabu Press, 2010.

Vines, Matthew. *God and the Gay Christian: The Biblical Case in Support of Same-Sex Relationships*. New York: Convergent Books, 2014.

von Goethe, Johann Wolfgang. *Reynard the Fox*. Translated by Hjalmar Hjorth Boyesen. Scotts Valley, CA: CreateSpace Independent Publishing Platform, 2015.

Wall, Robert W. with Richard B. Steele. *1 & 2 Timothy and Titus*. The Two Horizons New Testament Commentary. Edited by Joel B. Green and Max Turner. Grand Rapids, MI/Cambridge, UK: William B. Eerdmans Publishing Company, 2012.

The Hobbit: An Unexpected Journey. Directed by Peter Jackson. Burbank, CA: Warner Bros. Pictures, 2012. DVD.

The Lord of the Rings: The Return of the King. Directed by Peter Jackson. Burbank, CA: New Line Cinema, 2003. DVD.

Zakovitch, Yair. "On the Ordering of Psalms as Demonstrated by Psalms 136-150." In *The Oxford Handbook of The Psalms.* Edited by William P. Brown, 214-28. Oxford: Oxford University Press, 2014.

Resource List

LGBTQ+ affirming theology that "unclobbers" the clobber passages:

Baldock, Kathy. *Walking the Bridgeless Canyon: Repairing the Breach Between the Church and the LGBT Community*. Reno, NV: Canyonwalker Press, 2014.

Brownson, James V. Bible, Gender, *Sexuality: Reframing the Church's Debate on Same-Sex Relationships*. Grand Rapids, MI/Cambridge, UK: William B. Eerdmans Publishing Company, 2013.

Lee, Justin. *Torn: Rescuing the Gospel from the Gays-vs.-Christians Debate*. New York: Jericho Books, 2012.

Hartke, Austen. *Transforming: The Bible and the Lives of Transgender Christians*. Louisville, KY: Westminster John Knox Press, 2018.

Martin, Colby. *UnClobber: Rethinking Our Misuse of the Bible on Homosexuality*. Louisville, KY: Westminster John Knox Press, 2016.

Vines, Matthew. *God and the Gay Christian: The Biblical Case in Support of Same-Sex Relationships*. New York: Convergent Books, 2014.

Generally LGBTQ+ affirming theology:

Cheng, Patrick S. *Rainbow Theology: Bridging Race, Sexuality, and Spirit*. New York: Seabury Books, 2013.

Edman, Elizabeth M. *Queer Virtue: What LGBTQ People Know About Life and Love and How It Can Revitalize Christianity*. Boston: Beacon Press, 2016.

Lee, Deborah Jian. *Rescuing Jesus: How People of Color, Women, and Queer Christians are Reclaiming Evangelicalism*. Boston: Beacon Press, 2016.

Roberts, Mathias. *Beyond Shame: Creating a Healthy Sex Life on Your Own Terms*. Minneapolis, MN: Fortress Press, 2020.

Sanders, Cody J. *A Brief Guide to Ministry with LGBTQIA Youth*. Louisville, KY: Westminster John Knox Press, 2017.

Sanders, Cody J. *Queer Lessons for Churches on the Straight and Narrow: What All Christians Can Learn from LGBTQ Lives*. Macon, GA: Faithlab, 2013.

Smith, Kristian A. *Breaking all the Rules: An ancient framework for modern faith.* Cleveland, TN: Parson's Porch, 2020.

Robertson, Brandan, editor. *Our Witness: The Unheard Stories of LGBT+ Christians.* Eugene, OR: Cascade Books, 2018.

Robertson, Brandan. *True Inclusion: Creating Communities of Radical Embrace.* St Louis: Chalice Press, 2018.

Missions

Corbett, Steve and Brian Fikkert. *When Helping Hurts: How to Alleviate Poverty without Hurting the Poor… and Yourself.* Chicago: Moody Publishers, 2009.

Escobar, Kathy. *Down We Go: Living into the Wild Ways of Jesus.* Folsom, CA: Civitas Press, 2011.

Flemming, Dean. *Recovering the Full Mission of God: A Biblical Perspective on Being, Doing and Telling.* Downers Grove, IL: InterVarsity Press, 2013.

Lanier, Sarah A. *Foreign to Familiar: A Guide to Understanding Hot- and Cold-Climate Cultures.* Hagerstown, MD: McDougal Publishing, 2000.

Lupton, Robert D. *Toxic Charity: How Churches and Charities Hurt Those They Help* (And How to Reverse It). New York: HarperOne, 2011.

McKnight, John and Peter Block. *The Abundant Community: Awakening the Power of Families and Neighborhoods.* San Francisco: Beretta-Koehler Publishers, 2012.